Scottish Canoe Touring

An SCA canoe and kayak guide

Pesda Press

www.pesdapress.com

Proceeds from this guidebook will go to

The Andy Jackson Fund for Access

which is a registered Scottish Charity (SCO38644) that has been set up to:

• promote and protect access to water in Scotland for the population, by improving and enhancing physical access to waterways;

• advance the education and understanding of the public in the subject of responsible access to water in Scotland;

• promote for the benefit of the public the conservation, protection and improvement of the water environment and Scottish waters for their own sake, for the inspiration they give to humanity and for future generations, by promoting good practice by those taking access to water, by bringing to public attention environmentally harmful practices, and by practical intervention;

• improve public participation in healthy paddle sports and recreation by both promoting education of responsible access and physical improvements to improve access to water.

For further details, membership, etc, please send an SAE to:

> The Scottish Canoe Association
> Caledonia House
> South Gyle
> Edinburgh
> EH12 9DG

Or contact: www.CanoeScotland.com
Tel. 0131-317-7314

Front cover - Canoe in Mist - www.raygoodwin.com
Back cover - Loch Nevis - www.raygoodwin.com
Loch Lochy - www.raygoodwin.com
Loch Quoich - www.raygoodwin.com
Loch Loyal - www.standingwaves.co.uk

First published in Great Britain 2005 by Pesda Press
Galeri 22, Doc Victoria
Caernarfon, Gwynedd
LL55 1SQ, Wales
Reprinted with minor updates 2009

Printed in Poland, produced by Polskabook
Copyright © 2005 Scottish Canoe Association

ISBN 0-9547061-3-7

Foreword

A very warm welcome to this new canoeing guide to waters in Scotland!

Following on from the great success of 'Scottish White Water', now in its second edition, this book has pulled together routes on rivers, lochs, sea lochs, the canals and some stretches of coastline to complement the white water guides and offer easier and more sheltered water for the canoeist or kayaker.

The book is designed to both attract the novice paddler to Scotland, and offer different water and scenery to experienced canoeists. Many routes offer trips of more than one day's duration into our wonderful wilderness, one of the last wild outposts of Europe. In addition, there are details of some eleven expeditions which cross Scotland, and will test even the hardiest!

We also celebrate the introduction of the Land Reform Act, and the Access Code into Scotland in 2005, ensuring that access is now guaranteed for future generations. This is a fine and fitting result for those who have campaigned so hard over the years to clarify the situation, and of course it also sharpens up the responsibility of paddlers.

Thanks are due to the paddlers who gladly volunteered even their favourite and secret routes, following on from the tradition of the first guidebook. Some of these contributors have undertaken long expeditions in Scotland that should be the envy of all paddlers. As before, the income from sales of this book goes to the Andy Jackson Fund for Access charity which aims to support projects which promote and protect access to water in Scotland for the sport of canoeing.

This guide is a tribute to Andy Jackson, the SCA's former Access Officer who died so tragically at the end of 2004. Andy was the inspiration for 'Scottish White Water', and worked heroically to put it into print. He was personally responsible for enthusing many people to get on the water, and into a healthy and exciting pastime. We are indebted to both him and to Bridget Thomas, who edited the 'Scottish White Water Guide'.

I sincerely hope that all readers will enjoy their paddling and holidaying in Scotland, and our wonderful scenery and natural environment.

Eddie Palmer
Guidebook Editor

CONTENTS

Foreword 3
Using the Guide 6
Grading 8
River Levels 9
Hydro Campaign 9

Important Notice 9
Access 10
River Advisers 13
SCA Access Committee 13
Acknowledgements 14

Far North

Thurso

001 Upper Thurso 19
002 Middle Thurso 20
003 Lower Thurso 20
004 Loch Naver 21
005 River Naver 21
006 Kyle of Tongue 22
007 Loch Eriboll 23
008 Kyle of Durness 23
009 River Dionard 24
010 Loch Inchard 25
011 Loch Laxford 25
012 Handa Island 26

Ullapool

013 Kylesku Area 29
014 Stoer and Lochinver 30
015 The Inverpolly Lochs 31
016 Loch Sionascaig 32
017 Loch Veyatie and Fionn Loch 37
018 Loch Veyatie to River Polly 37
019 The Summer Isles 38
020 Little L. Broom and Gruinard Bay . . . 39
021 Loch Ewe 40
022 Loch Maree 40
023 Loch Gairloch 41
024 Loch Torridon 42

Bonar Bridge

025 Loch Shin 44
026 Lower River Oykel and Kyle of
    Sutherland 45
027 Dornoch Firth 45
028 Loch Fleet 46

Inverness

029 River Conon and Upper Lochs . . . 49
030 River Glass and River Beauly 50
031 Loch Monar 52
032 Loch Monar West to the Sea 53
033 Loch Mullardoch 54
034 Loch Affric and Loch Beinn a
    Mheadhoin 54
035 River Moriston 55
036 Loch Ness and River Ness 56

West

Kyle of Lochalsh

037 Crowlin Islands 61
038 Loch Kishorn and Loch Carron . . 61
039 Loch Duich, Loch Alsh and
    Loch Long 62
040 Loch Duich to Loch Hourn 63
041 Loch Hourn 64

Mallaig

042 Loch Nevis 66
043 Loch Morar 66
044 Loch Morar and Loch Nevis 67
045 Loch Shiel 68
046 Loch Shiel, River Shiel,
    Loch Moidart and Loch Eilt 73
047 Loch Moidart 74
048 Loch Sunart 75

Fort William

049 Loch Quoich, Upper River Garry
    and Loch Garry 80
050 Loch Oich and Loch Lochy 81
051 Loch Arkaig 81
052 River Lochy 82
053 Loch Laggan and Loch Spean . . . 83
054 Loch Treig 84
055 Loch Linnhe 85
056 Loch Leven 85
057 Rannoch Moor – Lochs Bà and
    Laidon, Rannoch Station 86
058 Loch Creran 87

Oban

059 Loch Etive 90
060 Lower Orchy 91
061 Loch Awe 92
062 Loch Avich 93
063 Loch Melfort and Nearby Islands . . 94

Lochgilphead

064 Loch Craignish 96
065 River Add and Loch Crinan 97
066 Crinan Canal 97
067 Tayvallich and Loch Sween 98
068 West Loch Tarbert 99

Cowal

069 Loch Fyne 102
070 Isle of Bute and Nearby Lochs . . 103
071 Lochs Long, Goil, Holy Loch
    and Gare Loch. 104
072 Loch Lomond 109
073 Loch Lomond, River Leven, Firth
    of Clyde and Loch Long. 111
074 Endrick Water 112

East

Moray and Grampian

075 River Nairn 119
076 Upper Findhorn. 120
077 Lower Findhorn. 122
078 Loch Ericht 123
079 River Spey. 123
080 River Deveron 128
081 River Don 130
082 River Dee 132

Tayside

083 Loch Rannoch. 139
084 Loch Tummel. 140
085 Lower River Tummel 140
086 Loch Daimh 145
087 Loch Lyon 146
088 Upper River Lyon. 146
089 Lower River Lyon. 147
090 Cononish, Fillan and Dochart . . 148
091 Loch Tay 150
092 River Tay 151
093 Firth of Tay. 155
094 Upper River Isla. 156
095 Lower River Isla. 158
096 Upper Shee Water. 160
097 Lower Ericht 161
098 River Earn 161

Angus

099 Lower North Esk 166
100 Upper South Esk 168
101 Lower South Esk 169
102 Dean Water. 171
103 Lunan Water 172

Fife

104 River Eden. 176
105 Loch Leven 181
106 River Leven 181

Central

107 Balquhidder to Loch Lubnaig. . . 187
108 Loch Achray, Loch Venachar
    and River Teith. 189
109 Loch Ard and River Forth. 191
110 River Devon 192
111 River Avon. 194
112 Union Canal 195
113 Forth and Clyde Canal. 196

South

Ayrshire

114 River Ayr 201
115 Loch Doon 203
116 River Doon 203

The Clyde Valley

117 Upper Clyde 206
118 Lower Clyde 207

Dumfries and Galloway

119 Luce Bay 211
120 Isle of Whithorn and Garlieston . . 211
121 Gatehouse of Fleet 212
122 Brighouse Bay, Kirkcudbright Bay . 212
123 Rivers Ken, Dee and Loch Ken. . 217
124 Auchencairn Bay, Orchardton
    Bay and Rough Firth 219
125 Lower Nith and Nith Estuary . . . 220
126 River Annan. 221

Borders

127 River Tweed. 225
128 River Teviot 229

Cross-Scotland Routes

A   Laxford Bridge to Bonar Bridge . 234
B   Inverkirkaig to Bonar Bridge . . . 235
C   Loch Maree to Conon Bridge . . 236
D   Great Glen (Caledonian Canal) . 236
E   Loch Nevis to Great Glen 239
F   Loch Morar to Great Glen 240
G   Kinlochleven to Perth 240
H   Loch Long to Stirling 242
I   Loch Long to River Forth and
    Stirling. 243
J   Glasgow to Edinburgh 243
K   Solway Firth to Berwick 244

Index 245

Using the Guide

This guide has been written primarily with the needs of the kayaker or canoeist in mind, who is looking for water to paddle on in Scotland, and is either new to the country, or searching for areas of Scotland new to them. It will also offer useful information to the experienced open canoeist who is seeking a length of water to travel on, perhaps for several days. The main aim of the guide is to help paddlers to get out safely into the countryside and on to water, with a minimum of fuss, and with basic helpful information.

It does not include white water paddling of grade 3 and above, except for some stretches of river where such rapids are easily portaged, or carried around. The 'Scottish White Water' publication describes these other rivers.

Types of Water

 Canals, slow-moving rivers and small inland lochs which are placid water, and easy to cope with.

 Large inland lochs, still with no current or tide, but which in high winds can produce large waves.

 Large rivers, where flood conditions can make paddling difficult, and requiring a higher level of skill. The rivers in this guide have grade 1 and 2 rapids.

 Estuaries and sea lochs, where the direction of the tide is all-important, and usually cannot be paddled against.

 Open sea, safer coastal routes suitable for placid water touring kayaks and canoes **(in calm, stable weather).**

The text points out the individual difficulties of the various waters. Readers with little experience are urged to look at (inspect) any water they are uncertain of, and to have access to up-to-date weather information. The mountains and lochs of Scotland are subject to frequent, sudden and local changes in weather due to the topography and prevailing weather patterns, and these should be regarded with great respect.

The guide is not intended for paddling generally on the sea in sea kayaks, which is outside its scope, although some popular coastal trips are included, where open canoes have been used frequently. Particular attention should be paid to weather forecasts when deciding whether to undertake one of these journeys.

Portages

 Portaging, is the carrying of canoes. Portage distances have been restricted to the occasional 100m or so, around rapids, canal locks etc. unless specifically mentioned. These portages are generally along the length of the waterway, that is downstream, not over heights.

 Beware! This icon indicates that there are isolated dangers that are described in more detail in the text. These should be carefully identified and evaluated by the reader.

Expedition Routes

 Some of the five geographical sections also contain some suggested **expedition routes**. Only bare details are included, as good planning and provisioning would be required, with the ability to survive in the outdoors for several days. Where routes cross the watershed, fairly near to the west coast, severe weather conditions can be encountered. Portages are often long and hard, both in terms of length, and height required, and thought should be given to support teams, and the means of communication with them.

Maps

 Indicates the numbers of the Ordnance Survey 1:50,000 **Landranger Series** needed to cover the route described.

Grades

 On rivers the grades of water are indicated using the international standard (see over). **2** would indicate grade 2 sections. **1-2** means harder than 1 but easier than 2. **1/2** means that stretches of 1 and stretches of 2 may be encountered. **(3)** would indicate an isolated short stretch of grade 3 that could be avoided by portaging.

River Grading

Rivers are graded in difficulty by an agreed international standard, and a simplified version is quoted here.

Grade 1 Easy. Occasional small rapids or riffles, waves regular and low. Most appropriate course, with deepest water, easy to see from canoe or kayak and steer down. Obstacles e.g. pebble banks, very easy to see. Presents really no problems to paddlers able to steer canoes and kayaks. Steering is needed, especially on narrow rivers.

Grade 2 Medium. Fairly frequent rapids, usually with regular waves, easy eddies, and small whirlpools and boils. Course generally easy to recognise, but may meander around gravel banks and trees etc. Paddlers in kayaks may get wet, those in open canoes much less so.

Grade 3 Difficult. Rapids numerous, and can be continuous. Course more difficult to see and decide, landing to inspect may be wise. Drops may be high enough not to see water below, with high and irregular waves, broken water, eddies and whirlpools/boils.
There is no water with rapids of above grade 3 advised in this guide. Where there are grade 3 rapids, avoiding or portaging is always possible.

Grade 4 Very Difficult. Long and extended stretches of rapids with high, irregular waves, difficult broken water, strong eddies and whirlpools. Course often difficult to recognise. High falls, inspection from bank nearly always necessary.

Grade 5 Exceedingly Difficult. Long and unbroken stretches of white water with individual features, and routes, very difficult to see. Many submerged rocks, high waterfalls, falls in steps, very difficult whirlpools and very fast eddies. Previous inspection absolutely necessary, risk of injury, swims always serious.

Grade 6 Absolute limit of difficulty. All previous mentioned difficulties increased to limit of practicability. Definite risk to life.

River Levels

In this guide, an indication is given of a suitable level to paddle by simple viewing on-site, for example 'if the rocks are covered downstream from the bridge'. Most 'flatter rivers' can be easily seen from a road or bridges, and judgements on level are reasonably easy to make by the individual.

The SCA website www.CanoeScotland.com also has an invaluable service offered together with SEPA (the Scottish Environmental Protection Agency) and Visit Scotland, of current, live river levels from gauges on mostly the smaller rivers. Common sense will aid the paddler to make judgements on the levels in the larger rivers. For example, if several tributaries of the Tay are 'huge', then within a few hours, the Tay itself will also be very high.

Hydro Campaign

For details of the comprehensive policy of the Scottish Canoe Association on renewable energy and its effects, see the SCA website at www.canoescotland.com. This policy has been widely consulted in recent years, and is greatly expanded from just consideration of hydro-electricity projects.

IMPORTANT NOTICE – DISCLAIMER

Canoeing and kayaking are healthy outdoor activities which always carry some degree of risk, as they involve adventurous travel, often away from habitation. Guidebooks give an idea of where to access a river, where to egress, the level of difficulty, and the nature of the hazards to be encountered. However, the physical nature of river valleys changes over time, water levels vary considerably with rain, and features such as weirs, walls and landings are changed by man. Trees block rivers, and the banks erode, sometimes quickly. Coastal sections, sea lochs, and large inland lochs are subject to the effect of tides and weather.

This guidebook is no substitute for inspection, personal risk assessment, and good judgement. The decision of whether to paddle or not, and any consequences arising from that decision, must remain with the individual paddler.

Access

The Land Reform (Scotland) Act 2003 now gives a clear framework for everybody to enjoy outdoor sports and activities. The Scottish Canoe Association and Scottish Natural Heritage, the relevant government agency, have produced a leaflet outlining both rights, and, as importantly, responsibilities (reproduced below).

It is important that everybody realises the two-way responsibility inherent in this Act, one of the best in Europe. Much of this is common sense, so overall... think!

There is now a statutory right of access to most land and inland water in Scotland. The Scottish Outdoor Access Code explains how to do this.

Enjoying responsible access on land

Access disputes have often arisen over either vehicle parking, or crossing land to water. Respect people's privacy by staying away from houses and private gardens – access rights do not apply here. Be discreet when either changing, or going to the toilet. If you are wild camping, choose a spot well away from roads and buildings, and be sure to remove all traces of your camp. You are able to camp, for example, in small numbers, for two to three nights. Do not use road lay-bys, or car parks.

Access rights do not apply to motorised transport – do not use private (usually estate) roads without permission, and do not drive over rough country, as much environmental damage might occur. Take care with parking, and do not block access or tracks or farm gates. You do, however, have a right, when not interfering with other people's livelihood or pleasure, to walk with a canoe from the road to the river or loch. Obviously, don't damage walls, fences, hedges or gates. Try and avoid animals and growing crops by keeping to the edge of fields, watch for any advice signs, and follow any reasonable guidance given.

Enjoying responsible access to water

Access rights apply to inland water such as rivers, lochs, canals, and reservoirs (with regard to the latter, the provision of access to some will come with improved water treatment at plants in 2005/6).

- Respect the needs of anglers by avoiding rods, lines, and other tackle. When close to anglers, keep noise and disturbance to a minimum.

- Care for the environment. Do not disturb wildlife, plants or your surroundings. Do not pollute the water, and report any pollution or suspicious activity.

- Rivers - Watch out for anglers, pass with least disturbance, and try and attract attention from upstream. If possible, wait for a signal to proceed and then follow a route down indicated, if it is safe and practicable to do so.

- Lochs - If anglers are present, try and keep a safe distance away to avoid any contact and disturbance. If the water is part of a commercial fishery, and intensively used, always attempt to speak to the land manager before going on the water.

- Sea - The sea is open and free, but take care to avoid disturbing nesting birds and other wildlife. For example, seals are nice to paddle near, but do not stress nursing mother seals and pups. There are many sea lochs in this guide where access poses no problem at all.

- Canals - Be aware of other traffic, and avoid motorised craft, who often do not have the draft (depth in the water) to avoid you. Access rights do not apply through locks and lifts. Follow any regulations and guidance, and if in doubt – ask. The canals in this guide have a very useful and informative website.

- Reservoirs and hydro schemes - Avoid going too close to water intake points, spillways, or other hydro infrastructure. Remember that water levels may change very quickly, and without warning.

Key Principles

Your main responsibilities are to:

- Care for the environment

- Take responsibility for your own actions

- Respect the interests of other people

These principles apply equally to canoeists, anglers, other water users, and land managers.

Local Authorities/National Park Authorities' Responsibilities

These Authorities have a responsibility to uphold access rights. If you feel you are challenged unreasonably, or otherwise prevented or discouraged from enjoying your access rights, you should report it to the relevant Access Officer (who will usually be employed in the Planning Department).

Land Managers' Responsibilities

Land Managers must respect access rights in their day-to-day work. Sometimes, for health and safety, or animal welfare reasons, they may have to lock gates or suggest alternative routes around areas of work. Co-operating with such situations helps land managers to work safely. Anglers are asked to respect access rights and to allow canoes to pass at the earliest opportunity.

Extra advice to canoeists

Please pay special regard to parking on rivers or lochs, and do not park in passing places on single-track roads. This causes much annoyance to local people. Remember that parking for a van and canoe trailer requires more space than for a small car, and park with consideration.

Whilst driving on single-track roads, pay heed to the good practice prevalent, and allow overtaking by faster traffic (you can incur penalties for obstruction if you do not do this!), and pull into passing places in good time, avoiding the need for any reversing of trailers.

For more information on the Act, the Access Code, and contact details for Access Officers:

         www.outdooraccess-scotland.com
         www.CanoeScotland.com

River Advisers

The major rivers in this guidebook have river advisers. They are happy to be contacted for information about likely river flows, any particular local access issues (avoiding the annoyance of other water-users), or new hazards. You can help them by reporting anything of note you find on your trip. Please remember that it is a voluntary service, and that river advisers have other jobs – be sensitive about the times you contact them. You are under no obligation to contact a river adviser, but planning a long trip with a large group might repay itself by contacting them. The major touring rivers can come under particular pressure at times. There is a list of river advisers on the SCA website www.CanoeScotland.com.

SCA Access Committee

The aim of this guidebook and the aims of the Access Committee are the same: to assist you to enjoy Scottish water. Broadly this gives us two areas of work. The practical day-to-day resolution of local issues is complemented by the provision of information, advice and other action to promote enjoyment of the countryside.

The Land Reform (Scotland) Act and the Access Code which came into force on February 9th 2005 have enabled the Committee to take a much broader view of our work. When arguing for our rights we now have a legal framework which we helped to write. The Access Code provides the framework to resolve the practical day-to-day issues that will occur on and off the water. It forms the basis of the Paddlers' Code and our negotiations with land managers and local authorities, particularly their Access Officers. These negotiations range from sensitive areas on the river to parking, toilets, information signs, camping provision, gates and fences etc. Other important areas of negotiation include improving access to existing hydro schemes and limiting the damage caused by new ones. All is aimed at facilitating access to Scotland's water and giving you the information you may need to use access responsibly.

This legal right enables us to look much more widely at helping paddlers enjoy the Scottish countryside. Using our Environmental Policy we promote canoeing as an environmentally sound as well as healthy activity – an ideal recreational activity. Come and join us.

Acknowledgements

Some of the waters in this book have been paddled by many people, and so three or four slightly different descriptions of the same river or loch have been helpful in order to get down on paper a rounded account of the enjoyment to be had. In some cases, there has only been a single account received, and there are still some rumoured expeditions which have been successfully completed! Thanks to all who contributed.

Duncan Black
Fred Connacher
Mary Connacher
Paul Cromey
Roland Denereaz
Chris Dickinson
Anna Gordon
Steve Hankin
Richard Hathaway
John Hattersley
Paul Jackson
Stuart Marshall
Geoff Miller
Eddie Palmer
Dave Rossetter
Graeme Smith
Bridget Thomas
Malcolm Wield
Staff of YMCA Lakeside, Windermere
Members of the Open Canoe Sailing Group

Special thanks regarding the compilation of this guide to:
Mary Connacher, Eddie Palmer, John Picken, Stuart Smith, and Bridget Thomas.

Photos have been acknowledged in the captions, apart from those used on the section contents pages. They are:

Far North:	Wilderness Systems/White Water Consultancy
West:	Perception/Helen Metcalfe
East:	www.raygoodwin.com
Central:	www.standingwaves.co.uk
South:	Perception/Neilson
Cross-Scotland:	Perception/Helen Metcalfe

Far North

Far North

Thurso

001 Upper Thurso 19
002 Middle Thurso 20
003 Lower Thurso 20
004 Loch Naver 21
005 River Naver 21
006 Kyle of Tongue 22
007 Loch Eriboll 23
008 Kyle of Durness 23
009 River Dionard 24
010 Loch Inchard 25
011 Loch Laxford 25
012 Handa Island 26

Ullapool

013 Kylesku Area 29
014 Stoer and Lochinver 30
015 The Inverpolly Lochs 31
016 Loch Sionascaig 32
017 Loch Veyatie and Fionn Loch . . 37
018 Loch Veyatie to River Polly 37
019 The Summer Isles 38
020 Little L. Broom and Gruinard Bay . . . 39
021 Loch Ewe 40
022 Loch Maree 40
023 Loch Gairloch 41
024 Loch Torridon 42

Bonar Bridge

025 Loch Shin 44
026 Lower River Oykel and Kyle of
    Sutherland 45
027 Dornoch Firth 45
028 Loch Fleet 46

Inverness

029 River Conon and Upper Lochs . 49
030 River Glass and River Beauly . . 50
031 Loch Monar 52
032 Loch Monar West to the Sea . . . 53
033 Loch Mullardoch 54
034 Loch Affric and Loch Beinn a
    Mheadhoin 54
035 River Moriston 55
036 Loch Ness and River Ness 56

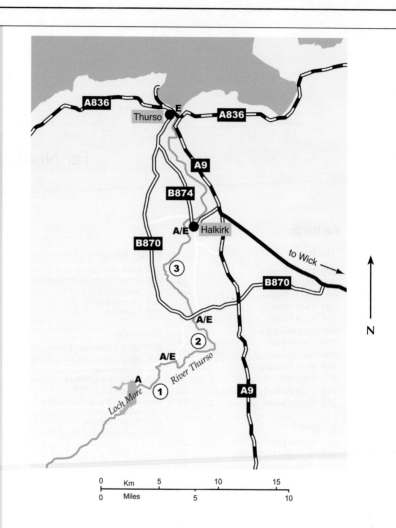

Thurso

001 Upper Thurso 19
002 Middle Thurso 20
003 Lower Thurso 20

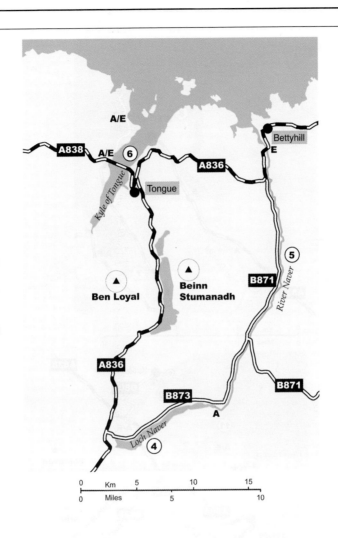

Thurso - continued

004 Loch Naver. 21
005 River Naver 21
006 Kyle of Tongue 22

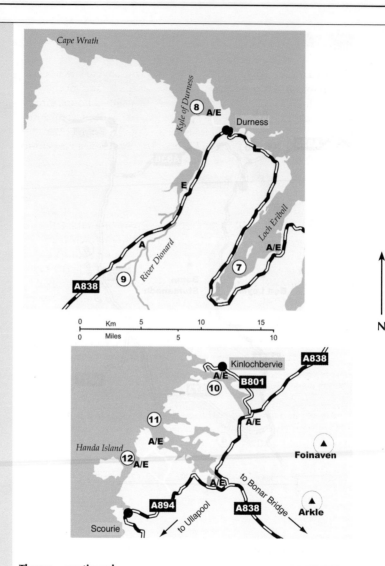

Thurso - continued

007 Loch Eriboll 23   010 Loch Inchard 25
008 Kyle of Durness 23   011 Loch Laxford 25
009 River Dionard. 24   012 Handa Island 26

Thurso

This area has two main towns, Wick and Thurso, the latter best known for its surfing beaches. Caithness is flatter and more agricultural than its western and indeed southern neighbours, often a surprise for visitors. The east coast has a string of pretty fishing villages, and inland is the famous 'Flow Country', one of the largest areas of blanket bog in Europe. To the west is a vast empty land, with no settlements of any size.

Upper Thurso 001

Introduction This is the most north-easterly river on the UK mainland, and flows gently from a bog south-west of Thurso town. It is probably little paddled, has quiet rather than spectacular scenery, and is also a popular salmon river. The river is small until it passes through Loch More, which can be reached by a public road from the A895, the main spine road running north up to Thurso. There is one stretch of continuous rapids, the Dirlot Gorge (start at 117481), which could be avoided by starting at Westerdale, plus two other short stretches. The guide to the river is presented in three sections.

LENGTH	**5km**
OS	**11**
GRADE	**1**

Water Level   There is a gauge in Halkirk, 24 inches is a good level.

Access Road access and parking are easy, as this is a quiet part of the country. This first section can be accessed at the end of Loch More (083461), with egress further down the road (117481).

Campsites & accommodation Two sites in Thurso, a fairly major town.

Description
Km

0   Bridge at Lochmore Cottage, exit from loch.
      The small Loch Beg follows.

3.5   Strathmore Lodge on left bank.

5   River leaves road. Take out here (117481), or carry on down
      next section.

002 Middle Thurso – Dirlot Gorge

LENGTH **12km**
OS **11**
GRADE **2/3**

Access Start at spot on minor road (117481). Egress at Westerdale Bridge, B870 (131518).

Description

Km

0   River leaves road. Series of small drops.

1   Dirlot Castle ruin on left bank. Start of rapids, small ledges and bedrock rapids.

7   Cemetery on bank, last rapid, large rock in middle.

8   Farm road bridge.

9   Two brochs on right bank.

12   Dale Moss bog on right side.
     Broch on right followed by road bridge, B870 – Westerdale.

003 Lower Thurso

LENGTH **25km**
OS **11**
GRADE **1-2**

Access Westerdale bridge (131518), egress Thurso road bridge (118681).

Description

Km

0   B870 road bridge and Westerdale hamlet. Rapid below bridge.
     More small hamlets follow on both banks.

9   Railway bridge – Georgemas Junction Station is 3km to right, where the rail line divides, with branches to both Wick and Thurso. Rapids start for next 2km.

10   Weir.

10.5 B874 road bridge, and Halkirk village.

11   Weir. Braal Castle.

17   Rail bridge.

21.5 Weir.

25   Thurso road bridge (118681).

Loch Naver 004

Introduction This area of the far north is wild and spectacular, and mainly unexplored by paddlers. The scenery is very fine, and people few and far between, apart from anglers.
Loch Naver runs for 9km east from Altnaharra on the A836, a long and tortuous single-track road. To the south are the imposing crags of Ben Klibreck.

LENGTH	**9**km
OS	**16**
GRADE	-

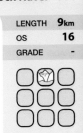

Access The loch (5735 to 6638) can be accessed from the north side off the B873, and offers a wilderness paddle.

River Naver 005

Introduction The river is very shallow and stony, with frequent minor rapids, and quite dangerous due to many trees in high water. Strathnaver is of historic interest, being the scene of some of Scotland's most notorious land clearances in the 19th Century.

LENGTH	**30**km
OS	**10/16**
GRADE	**2**

Water Level Drive along and have a look – the river comes up and down quickly.

Access The B873 road follows the river all the way down, and so access on and off is quite easy. Access at the top, either off a farm road to just where the river leaves Loch Naver (669378), or off the B873 (676386). Final egress at A836 road bridge just before Bettyhill (710602).

Campsites & accommodation There is a campsite at Bettyhill, where the Naver joins the sea.

006 Kyle of Tongue

LENGTH	**6km**
OS	**10**
GRADE	-

Introduction The north coast is an extremely dangerous and exposed one, offering sheltered touring in only a couple of places. The Kyle is a beautiful place, with villages around the western entrance from the sea.

Access The A838 crosses part of the Kyle by a causeway. Access either off this via two parking places (581586), or by the minor road north, up the west side, to Talmine and Portvasgo (Talmine Bay 586627).

Campsites & accommodation There is a small site at Talmine, near to the beach.

Description Talmine has a safe anchorage, much used by yachts coming 'around the corner' making for Orkney, plus a village store and a campsite. In summer, this area is swarmed over by camper vans from Europe, who obviously have a good guidebook!
The Rabbit Islands offshore are good to make for in settled weather, with its own population of seals, but please do not disturb – this is a wild area. In very calm weather even Eilean nan Ron could be attempted. This island used to be inhabited and has ruined houses. In the 1970s a group of hippies repopulated it for a few years.
It is 7km from Talmine up the Kyle, under the causeway, to Tongue itself. Both Ben Loyal and Ben Hope are visible, usually, to the south.
The islands and coves at the entrance to the Kyle are frequently visited by whales and otters.

Loch Eriboll 007

Introduction This is the only other part of the north coast offering anything to the non-sea kayaker, which are the lochs of Eriboll and the Durness area.

LENGTH	**20km**
OS	**9**
GRADE	-

Access From the A838 on the western side of the loch, near to where a burn enters the loch at its head (391547), and at the car park above the beach at Traigh na h-Uamhag (443655).

Campsites & accommodation Durness, 20km away.

Description The inner part of Loch Eriboll can be sheltered from the weather, and a trip can be undertaken either from the head of the loch or near its mouth. (Access formerly from the east side of the loch is no longer practicable due to a fish farm.) At the head is a tidal lagoon of Lochan Havurn, and sandy beaches. The west side is 9km up to the beach open to the sea. The island of Eilean Choraidh sits in the middle of the loch.

Other important points It is about 6km around the rocky headland to the west to the first beach near to Durness (Traigh na h-Uamhag), *but this is fully exposed to the open sea.*
Durness offers more possibilities - 1.5km round to the Smoo caves, where you can pay to enter, being taken in by a rubber dinghy, and a further 2km out to various islands, Eilean Hoan being the largest.

Kyle of Durness 008

Introduction A pleasant area to spend a day, with the village of Durness and the 'craft village' of Balnakeil rather incongruously based in a World War 2 military base. Minibus trips can be made to Cape Wrath (the only way to reach it, apart from by kayak).

LENGTH	**16km**
OS	**9**
GRADE	-

Access From the A838 down to the coast at Balnakeil village (391687), or from the same road as it skirts the eastern side of the Kyle (3865).

Campsites & accommodation At Durness.

Description To the west, launching west of the dunes of Faraid Head at Balnakeil gives access to Eilean Dubh, and then round into the Kyle of Durness. This is a pleasant but tidal estuary which empties at low water. It is 8km up to the head of the Kyle. A ferry crosses halfway up, to take passengers over towards a minibus on the west side heading for Cape Wrath. Offshore here can be dangerous, as it is an RAF bombing range, to the annoyance of sea kayakers.

009 River Dionard

LENGTH **5**km
OS   **9**
GRADE**1/2 (3-)**

Introduction A small river giving some different paddling in the area, flowing down the wide Strath Dionard, with mountains either side. Mostly grade 1 and 2, but the little gorge near the end might be a touch harder.

Water Level The river needs to obviously have enough water in to paddle under the road bridge near the end. This is also a good place to inspect the rapids and small drops.

Access Follow the A838 south up the strath from the head of the Kyle, passing a bridge over the river after 1km. In another 3km, at a house called Carbreck (333593), a track leaves on the left, reaching the river after 1km (338586). Parking is easy on rough ground, egress is best on the right, 1km after reaching the tidal Kyle (372634).

Campsites & accommodation At Durness.

Description The river starts with occasional easy rocky rapids and fast bends. At one point it obviously narrows, and becomes a touch harder with a few drops, dropping faster under the road bridge, and then suddenly coming to an end. The Kyle is sandy underneath, and egress is to the right onto the road.

Loch Inchard 010

Introduction Loch Inchard is the first inlet coming south from Cape Wrath, and offers the first shelter for shipping.

LENGTH	**12**km
OS	**9**
GRADE	-

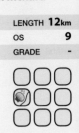

Access From Kinlochbervie, a small fishing port (221563), 6km along a narrow road from the A838 at Rhiconich, or from Rhiconich (255523) itself.

Campsites & accommodation At Durness to the north, or Scourie, 15km south.

Description It is 6km up to Rhiconich, and the entrance from the sea is very Norwegian fjord-like. Kinlochbervie stands in a wonderfully sheltered position, in a side loch off to the north, with port facilities for yachts and fishing boats, and shops etc. It's possible, in very calm weather, to launch on the west side of the village into Loch Clash, and paddle up the coast for 3km, within various islands to the beach at Oldshoremore. The walk from the end of the minor road to the north, up to Sandwood Bay is very rewarding, to one of the most famous and deserted beaches in Scotland.

Loch Laxford 011

Introduction Loch Laxford is a wonderful area for exploring, and offers paddling in a sheltered loch in spectacular scenery. It was here some years ago that John Ridgeway set up his somewhat controversial outdoor school, featured in a TV series.

LENGTH	**18**km
OS	**9**
GRADE	-

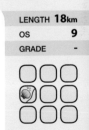

Access Launching can be had either at the head of the loch, off the main A838 road, at a boathouse where the road turns north away from the loch (228478); or at Fanagmore on the south side (178498), reached by minor roads.

Campsites & accommodation At Scourie, 10km south.

Description All of the islands, some of them very close to the shore with narrow passages are worth exploring, and seals and otters abound. The northern extension of Loch a Chad-Fi has the outdoor school at Ardmore – if landing, ask permission. A round day trip of some 18km can be worked out.

012 Handa Island

LENGTH **3km**
OS **9**
GRADE **-**

Description From Tarbet, 1.5km from Fanagmore, a trip out to Handa Island can be made, one of the premier bird sanctuaries for Scotland. Car parking can be had where the ferry leaves for Handa (164488). Please note that you will be asked to pay a landing fee on Handa which is owned by the Scottish Wildlife Trust (beach at 148476). The passage is normally a sheltered 1.5km. Many paddlers have circumnavigated Handa, but very calm conditions are needed for this.

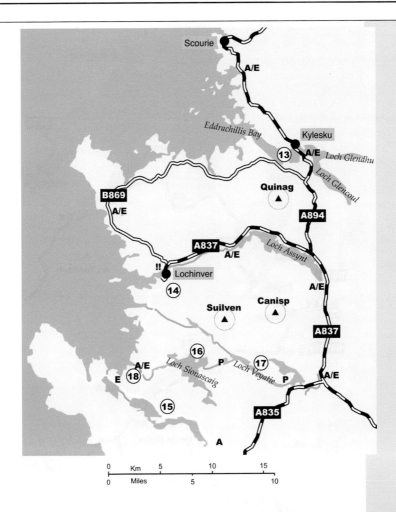

Ullapool

013 Kylesku Area. 29
014 Stoer and Lochinver 30
015 The Inverpolly Lochs 31
016 Loch Sionascaig 32
017 Loch Veyatie and Fionn Loch. 37
018 Loch Veyatie to River Polly. . . 37

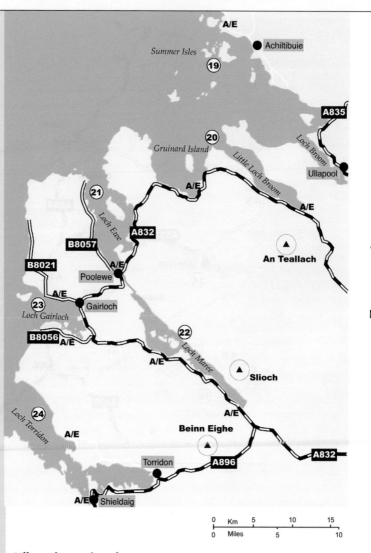

Ullapool - continued

019 The Summer Isles 38
020 Little L. Broom and Gruinard Bay 39
021 Loch Ewe 40

022 Loch Maree 40
023 Loch Gairloch. 41
024 Loch Torridon 42

Ullapool

This fishing village has expanded to be a major ferry port for Stornoway, and a centre for walking and climbing. It is always lively in the summer, and the Ceilidh Place Hotel offers frequent live music, and a bookshop, as well as political discussions. Ullapool is well served by hotels, B&Bs and restaurants.

Kylesku Area 013

Introduction Superlatives abound when discussing this part of Scotland, but it carries on with this superb area. I had a holiday with friends here some years ago where, in perfect summer conditions, we paddled open canoes on the sea for seven days running.

LENGTH **41**km
OS   **9/15**
GRADE   -

Access A base at Kylesku, on the A894 north-south main road offers the paddler many day trips. Kylesku still has its old ferry slipways, made redundant by the bridge built in the late 1970s, and the southerly one is conveniently near to the hotel (230338).

Campsites & accommodation Scourie, 15km north. Drumbeg, along the coast to the west, has a seasonal campsite.

Description The way inland and to the south explores Loch Glencoul, and at its head, the highest waterfall in Britain, Eas a Chual Aluinn (280278). The way in by canoe is much more pleasant than the quite rough and boggy walk 5km in from the road, where you end up seeing the top of the fall, but not the full extent of it! The head of the loch, inside Loch Beag, provides many sheltered picnic sites. If you make the trip on a wet day the waterfall is spectacular. The round trip from Kylesku is 13km.
Loch Glendhu to the east could be combined in a day out as well, 12km up here and back.
Out to sea, Eddrachillis Bay has many islands and sheltered waters. Loch a Chairn Bhain offers a first 6km of shelter. Going north, islands can be wound around as far as the tiny beach at Upper Badcall, which is a further 7.5-8km (153415).
West has more delights – possibly 8km (in a straight line) to the eastern side of Oldany Island. On the way, the fjord-like Loch na Droighniche (1634) and Loch Ardbhair (1633) after 3km. Then Loch Nedd, (1332) a further 5km round to its head amongst lush

woodland, and after that the useful Loch Dhrombaig (1133), with the village of Drumbeg, pub, and car parking, for a vehicle shuttle via the B869, one of Scotland's no-no roads for caravans. The coast after this becomes complicated and very indented, Culkein Drumbeg offering very sheltered but shallow anchorages for larger boats. It is not advised to go further around Oldany. The west side of the island is very exposed to the west, and the seas which come around the corner from the Point of Stoer, one of the west of Scotland's major headlands.

Overall, this part of the coast, both north and south of Kylesku, can offer a wonderful variety of day trips, or days of canoe-camping.

014 Stoer and Lochinver

LENGTH **72**km
OS   **15**
GRADE   -

Distances 30-35km of sea paddling, 10km loch, and 7km river.

Introduction This bay between the Point of Stoer and the headland of Rubha Coigach to the south provides a number of canoeing possibilities, with interesting indented fjord-like inlets, but obviously exposure seawards.

Access The A837 is a fast main road into Lochinver (European-funded, to move fish southwards quickly), but the minor roads both north and south from Lochinver are single-track, winding, and very slow, especially in summer.

Campsites & accommodation Clachtoll, Achmelvich and Achnahaird.

Description South from the Point of Stoer (well worth visiting for spectacular cliffs and the stack of Old Man of Stoer) is the Bay of Stoer (0328) at the village of Clachtoll, with a campsite, and then Achmelvich (058247), with its own sandy bay campsite. This is laidback summer holiday territory. Loch Roe, a fjord-like inlet, follows to the south. The headlands between the bays can be rounded, as always, in settled weather.

Lochinver is the main settlement, with its own sea loch, 4km out to Soyea Island at the mouth. The many possibilities inland from here are covered later in the guide. Loch Assynt, on the main road inland, offers a 10km trip over its length (2422 to 1625), with an extension down the River Inver flowing towards Lochinver...

however, beware, there is a short stretch of grade 3, a short gorge, and a weir before a final grade 5 drop just before the sea. Egress on right of river (123238) onto minor road (road bridge and foot-bridge signal this is coming up), after 5-6km.

Onwards south from Lochinver are more inlets and islands, offering more shelter from westerly or south-westerly winds. The coast road is a famous route of hairpins and steep gradients, banned to caravans, and difficult in places for trailers. Loch Kirkaig (0719) is pretty, and several other bays open up as minor burns reach the sea. It is a paddle of 9km over open sea to Achnahaird Bay, with a fabulous sandy beach on the peninsula to the south, and a large campsite (018136).

The Inverpolly Lochs 015

LENGTH	**13**km
OS	**15**
GRADE	**1**

Portages Two portages, one of which can be 1km.

Introduction Inland from Achnahaird is a string of lochs which gives a pleasant day trip, with the backdrop of the peaks of the Inverpolly Nature Reserve. Best from the furthest east, in a westerly direction to the sea (downhill), although it has been done in the other direction (with some hard portages). The trip gives even a beginner the sense of a true wilderness trip, but with the road virtually alongside for escape.

Water Level The small rivers between the three lochs can be dry in summer, but short rainstorms can bring the lochs and rivers up very quickly. Judge from the road.

Access From the single track road which leaves the A835 at Drumrunie, west to Achnahaird and Achiltibuie. Access at east end from road (139068), egress on to same road (039130).

Campsites & accommodation Achnahaird.

Description

Km

0   Start at easterly end of Loch Lurgainn. Parking on road in large passing-place (where climbers start out for Ben Mor Coigach) . This is some 3.5km on the road to Achiltibuie,

from where it leaves the A835. The burn then turns into the loch. There are spectacular mountains on both sides.

6   Short drop into Loch Bad na h'Achlaise, a very small loch. The loch bends to the right.

7   Fall into Loch Bad a Ghaill, easy short portage over rocks.

9.5   Start of the Abhainn Osgaig, 1.5km river down to next loch. Shallow, with gravel rapids. If portaging, follow right bank at first, over a high piece of land, then by bank of river, where lining down may be possible.

11   Loch Osgaig.

13   Egress, on to road (039130), where there is a parking place. The loch then empties into a very short and rough river down to the sea over 250m.

016 Loch Sionascaig

LENGTH   **9km**
OS   **15**
GRADE   -

Portages Northern access has a 0.5km portage. Southern access has a 200m portage.

Introduction A lovely loch in a wild setting, giving the impression of being miles from anywhere and takes the paddler into the heart of the Inverpolly National Nature Reserve.

Access This loch can be accessed from the minor, and very winding, coastal B road north from the Stac Polly area to Lochinver. (Be careful of taking trailers on this road, it has very tight corners in places, which are being gradually improved). There are two access points, the easiest being north of the valley of the River Polly, (082136), from the road to Loch na Dail, then upstream into the western arm of Loch Sionascaig. The other is 2km north (093151), along a path between Loch Cail an Uidhean and Loch Buine Moire, to Boat Bay on the main loch, a delightful enclosed bay with good campsites.
Be very careful with parking on this road as there are no obvious parking places!

Campsites & accommodation Wild sites abound. Achnahaird is the nearest formal site in this area.

The Sumer Isles - www.RayGoodwin.com

The Far North , Suilven in the background - www.RayGoodwin.com

Laxford Bridge - Inspirational Coaching

Portage on Cross-Scotland Route A - Inspirational Coaching

Loch Shin - Inspirational Coaching

Putting on below the Falls of Shin - Inspirational Coaching

Description The loch is 4.5km long and 3km wide, with Eilean Mor in the centre, again another good campsite. At the eastern end, a narrow gap with a short river leads upstream to Lochan Gainmeich, and Loch an Doire Dhuibh.

Loch Veyatie and Fionn Loch 017

LENGTH	**27**km
OS	**15**
GRADE	**1**

Portages Portage of a waterfall after Cam Loch.

Introduction Another true wilderness trip, but with really no difficulties, with great views of Suilven.

Access Road access from the A835, 2km from Ledmore Junction, where the A837 and A835 join. At this point, a tiny river flows under the road, just east of Elphin village (229120).

Campsites & accommodation No formal sites are near, although Achnahaird is west, and Kylesku is to the north. Wild sites on the trip.

Description The small river near to Elphin gives access to the area, rather than by the horrendous portage up the Kirkaig from the west. This gives entry to the Cam Loch, 3km long. Heading west, entry to Loch Veyatie is via a waterfall that will need portaging. Loch Veyatie is 7km long, and leads into the Uidh Fhearna, a short river, which in turn flows into Fionn Loch, 3.5km long. This route has the spectacular bulk of Suilven, one of Scotland's most recognisable mountains, to the north. The paddle in and back is well worthwhile.

Loch Veyatie to River Polly 018

LENGTH	**28**km
OS	**15**
GRADE	**1-2**

Portages Two portages, the first after Cam Loch, the other west out of Loch Veyatie, which is 2km including a short uphill, and a burn downhill.

Introduction An interesting variation on the two previous routes is a trip west, with a difficult portage, which has been done by kayak. (There are relatively few long trips going west on the west coast, due to the watershed being so near to the coast).

Access Access is via the A835 near to Elphin, as in Route 17 (229120); egress can be after Loch Sionascaig as in access to Route 016 (083135). If the full route is followed, the finish is at Achnahaird campsite (018136).

Campsites & accommodation Wild sites en route, with Achnahaird at the finish.

Description Take the route as described in Route 017. Then 5.5km down Loch Veyatie is a large bay on the left (west). Paddle up to the westerly end, and portage 250m north-west up to a burn leaving a tiny lochan. This is soon swollen by another burn leaving Loch a Mhadail. The burn flows for 1.5km down to Lochan na Claise, then by a very short burn down to the most easterly bay on Loch Sionascaig. The whole of the loch is then before you, and an exit can be made at the first access point in Route 16, or, more interestingly, down the River Polly (often very dry and rocky but great in spate, beware of fallen trees).
The Polly flows down a fertile and wooded valley 3.5km to the sea at Polly Bay, near to some holiday lodges. There is no road access here, apart from the private estate road, but the trip is improved by paddling out to Achnahaird Bay and campsite, some 5km around a headland. In calmish weather, this is often a flat paddle, due to the shelter from prevailing winds.
This whole trip is some 28km minimum paddling, and although could possibly be done in a long day, this would not give the experience of camping in this area.

019 The Summer Isles

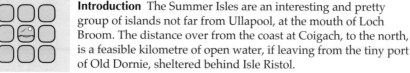

LENGTH **16km**
OS   **15**
GRADE   -

Distances A round paddle of 16km circumnavigates both of the main islands.

Introduction The Summer Isles are an interesting and pretty group of islands not far from Ullapool, at the mouth of Loch Broom. The distance over from the coast at Coigach, to the north, is a feasible kilometre of open water, if leaving from the tiny port of Old Dornie, sheltered behind Isle Ristol.

Access A minor road circles the Rubha Coigach peninsula, from either Achnahaird or Achiltibuie, and Old Dornie is 1km off this road (982112).

Campsites & accommodation Altandhu, Polbain, and Achiltibuie all have accommodation. The nearest campsite is at Achnahaird, just over the peninsula.

Description The usual destinations are Tanera Mor, the largest island, and Tanera Beg, its neighbour. The usual precaution of settled weather is a must here... several times in the past, groups have left the mainland in calm conditions, only to be benighted by a change in the weather.

Tanera Mor is the only permanently inhabited island; on its east side is the natural harbour 'The Anchorage', with a jetty to the south, a fish farm in the centre, and a landing, post office and coffee shop to the north. On the north-west corner of the island is an interesting little cove, with a narrow slot through to the strait between the two islands. Tanera Beg has a fabulous small gap between it and Eilean Fada Mor to the north (unfortunately now nearly filled by another fish farm, and a boom). The entrance from the south has a coral sand bottom, clearly visible at low tide. It is an undoubted privilege to paddle here. The circumnavigation of both islands is about 16km. The other islands are not mentioned because they are really a sea kayaker's domain.

Little Loch Broom and Gruinard Bay 020

Distances A trip of 24km can be had in Little Loch Broom, and 4.5km in Gruinard Bay.

LENGTH	**29**km
OS	**19**
GRADE	-

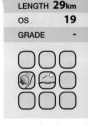

Introduction This area offers some paddling, much as any part of this coast. The view to the south of Little Loch Broom is dominated by the massive bulk of An Teallach, one of the largest Munros. The view to the north, once out of the loch, is filled with the Summer Isles.

Access From the A832 coastal main road, access on to Little Loch Broom near its head (0888); from the same road, on to the beach at Gruinard Bay via a parking place (953900).

Campsites & accommodation Laide, west side of Gruinard Bay.

Description It is 12km from the head of Little Loch Broom out to where the ferry crosses over to the alternative community of Scoraig, now also linked by a 4-wheel drive track.

The headland of Stattic Point round to Gruinard Bay can be too windy, but the bay is worth seeing for the beach at its head. The island of Gruinard, once famous as the 'anthrax island' due to biological experiments during World War 2, is now clear, and can be visited, 1.5km off Mungasdale Bay to the east, and 3km from the large beach.

021 Loch Ewe

LENGTH **24km**
OS **19**
GRADE **-**

Introduction Loch Ewe is large and exposed to the north-west. It is also a live training area for warships, which can speed in and out of the loch, a facility which has been kept since World War 2 when Atlantic convoys gathered here.

Access From Poolewe on A832 (860810).

Campsites & accommodation At Poolewe.

Description Poolewe at the inner end is sheltered, and also near to the Inverewe Gardens, with semi-tropical plants and well worth visiting. The loch is some 12km long, and rather feature-less, although the old wartime fortifications on the west side at the end of the road are worth a look.

022 Loch Maree

LENGTH **40km**
OS **19**
GRADE **-**

Distances A 40km round trip.

Introduction Paddling on Loch Maree has been contentious in the past; the access situation has now been smoothed over by the new Act in Scotland. Canoeists are requested now to go first to the Loch Maree Hotel and speak to the owner, so that he can give information on which islands should be avoided. This will be because of nesting birds such as Great Northern Divers. This process is a simple and helpful one, which will avoid any conflict between recreationists, land managers and conservation bodies.

Access From the west side of the loch, from the A832, at or near to the Loch Maree Hotel (915705), or from a parking place near to the southern end of the loch (001650).

Campsites & accommodation At Kinlochewe or Poolewe.

Description The loch is yet another Scottish gem, being 20km long, with a variety of interesting islands in the centre where it is 3.5km wide. Slioch dominates the skyline to the north-east, but the whole area is surrounded by breathtaking mountains. Loch Maree is also the possible start to a west-east crossing of Scotland.

Loch Gairloch 023

LENGTH	**24km**
OS	**19**
GRADE	-

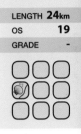

Distances A 24km round trip.

Introduction This loch is fairly isolated with regard to the coast north and south, but the shoreline of the loch is fairly long, with some interesting inlets. A good holiday can be had by using a centre such as the campsite at Poolewe, or one of the Gairloch ones, and exploring Lochs Ewe, Maree, Gairloch and Torridon. Inland there is a fabulous range of mountains.

Access From the A832 up the eastern side of the loch (8076), or the minor road which goes west from Gairloch village along the north shore.

Campsites & accommodation Around the loch, at Little Sands, Gairloch, Charlestown, or Kerrysdale.

Description From the northern entrance to the loch, Big Sand, on Caolas Beag (752788), gives access to the shallow sound between the mainland and the island of Longa (campsite also at Little Sand Farm). It is 5km along the north shore to Gairloch village, road alongside. The coast turns south, with a beach, headland, and 3km round to Charlestown village. In the south-east corner are the useful sheltered inlets of Loch Kerry and Loch Shieldaig, with islets and wooded shores. To the west again, 4km round from Charlestown, is Badachro, well worth visiting for its friendly pub, and very sheltered anchorage behind Eilean Horrisdale. A trip 3km west from here could be made to Port Henderson, but this piece of coast is more exposed.

024 Loch Torridon

LENGTH **20km**
OS   **24**
GRADE   -

Distances A 20km round trip.

Introduction Torridon is another highly indented inlet, with an inner and outer loch, giving more possibilities in bad weather.

Access From the A896, which skirts the south side of the loch, Shieldaig being the first settlement (815536), and the minor road which hugs the north shore to Torridon village (899563).

Description Loch Torridon itself is open and exposed, with no road on its northern side. Loch Diabeg is a small inlet, with the village of Lower Diabeg (798599), and access to the water. It is 4.5km across to Loch a Chracaich on the south shore, where there is a road. The scenery is more barren, and countryside more isolated than the former sections to the north. Loch Torridon narrows just inshore from here, and Loch Shieldaig opens up to the south, 5km up to Shieldaig village. If paddling here, the entrance to Upper Loch Torridon will have been passed, less than half a kilometre wide, to the north. The upper loch is 8km long, ending at Torridon village. There are roads on both north and south shores, so there are possibilities here for sheltered paddling in breathtaking mountain scenery. More inlets on the south shore.

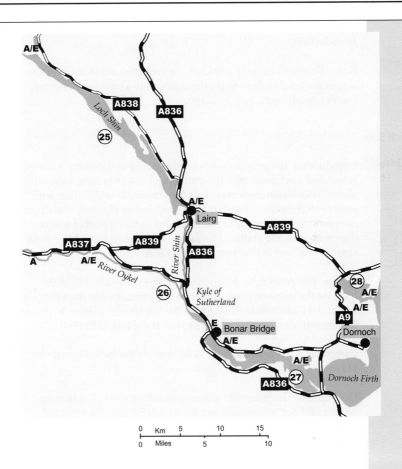

Bonar Bridge

025 Loch Shin 44
026 Lower River Oykel and Kyle of
     Sutherland 45
027 Dornoch Firth 45
028 Loch Fleet 46

Introduction

Bonar Bridge does have a bridge… a very important road bridge across the tidal Kyle of Sutherland, and it is a meeting of routes, but not much more, just a village.

025 Loch Shin

LENGTH **28km**

OS   **16**

GRADE   -

Introduction It's good to say something nice about every piece of water, but Loch Shin tries the patience! It is a very long loch, with almost no redeeming features, as the scenery is undulating with commercial forestry, much of it cleared and re-planted, with high deer fences. It is known to paddlers due to being part of one of the cross-Scotland routes. The loch is much used for fishing from small boats, and is also very midge-ridden.

Access The A838 runs down most of the north-east side of the loch. At the southern end, a dam blocks direct exit to the village of Lairg. Take out before the dam on the left (north) side on to one of the short tracks used by anglers to reach the loch (573075).

Campsites & accommodation Wild sites on the loch. Formal site at Lairg.

Description There are few features or settlements. A start may be had on Loch a Ghriama, north of Loch Shin, and connected, crossed by a bridge at the neck (390252). The A838 runs down the north-east side. Lairg is a pleasant village, only 11km from Bonar Bridge, with usual facilities.
A B-road down the west side of the River Shin (grade 1-3), leads to the grade 4 Falls of Shin (Visitor centre and café - 576991), well worth visiting in autumn to see the many salmon coming up to spawn, and jumping the falls.

Lower River Oykel and Kyle of Sutherland 026

Introduction This trip gives a fairly fast river experience in a flat-bottomed and agricultural valley, becoming an easy tidal paddle for those not used to large estuaries. Mountain scenery gives way to the Kyle, which is pretty and wooded.

LENGTH **28**km
OS **16/20/21**
GRADE **1-2**

Access From the A837 at Oykel Bridge, (386009) a minor road bridge 9km downstream (460013), and at Bonar Bridge on to the A9 (just upstream of bridge - 608922).

Campsites & accommodation At Lairg and Dornoch. The spectacular Youth Hostel at Carbisdale Castle overlooks the Kyle.

Description The Oykel provides 9km of paddling, to add on to a trip down the Kyle of Sutherland. It is a flattish river of grade 1-2, in a flat-bottomed valley, but with mountains to the north and south. It can also be the eastern end of a cross-Scotland route. The start is just below Oykel Bridge, where the river flows under the main A837 major east-west route. The high Falls of Oykel (grade 4-5) are just upstream. On the east side of the bridge is a track alongside the river, downstream, for launching. Downstream 9km is a first public road bridge, and the Oykel becomes tidal here, and usually known as the Kyle, offering a further 19km down to Bonar Bridge. The Cassley, a beautiful white water river, joins from the left 1.5km further on. Access and egress can be had after another 2.5km where the road is alongside. The Shin joins from the left at 12km, and then the main railway line to the north crosses the narrows at 13.5km. The Kyle has a widening out then a final narrow stretch before Bonar Bridge. The Dornoch Firth then commences, until the open sea.

Dornoch Firth 027

Distances 48km from Bonar Bridge to Dornoch and return.

LENGTH **48**km
OS   **21**
GRADE   -

Introduction A long, narrow firth with strong tides at the narrow parts, and large sandbanks. It is possible to reach Dornoch around Dornoch Point in settled weather. Dornoch is renowned for good weather in summer, and has extensive beaches and sand dunes.

Access From the A9, both sides of the firth. The north side is easier due to railway line on south side. East of Bonar Bridge (6190), and from Newton Point (711877).

Campsites & accommodation At Lairg and Dornoch.

Description It is 4km down from Bonar Bridge to Wester and Easter Fearn Points on the south bank, separated from a high point with Dun Creich fort on the north side by only 200m of water. 6 more km to a turn to the south at Ardmore Point, and 4km further on to the Dornoch Firth Bridge. The old ferry terminals are on points just before the bridge. It is 6km on to the open sea at Dornoch Point, with Tain to the south, and the town of Dornoch 2km along the coast to the north.

028 Loch Fleet

LENGTH	8km
OS	21
GRADE	-

Distances 8km round trip.

Introduction This sheltered estuary lies to the north of Dornoch, and is a delightful, quiet wildlife habitat.

Access The A9 runs across The Mound, a causeway at the landward end of the estuary. Minor roads run out on both sides of the stretch of water, offering easier parking, at Skelbo Castle to the south (794954), and Littleferry Pier (805956) to the north.

Campsites & accommodation At Dornoch and Embo, just to the south.

Description The loch is only 4km long from The Mound, a causeway which the A9 road to the north crosses, to its mouth at Littleferry, the old ferry crossing in former times. The loch virtually dries out at low tide, but would be of interest to birdwatchers. From Loch Fleet to the north is the east coast of Sutherland, and the east Caithness coast, with rocky cliffs, no large inlets, and very little shelter.

Other important points To the south of this area lies the Cromarty Firth, large, and partially industrial (it is used as a storage place for disused or de-commissioned oil rigs), the Moray Firth, used by large ships, and the Beauly Firth, very dry at low tide.

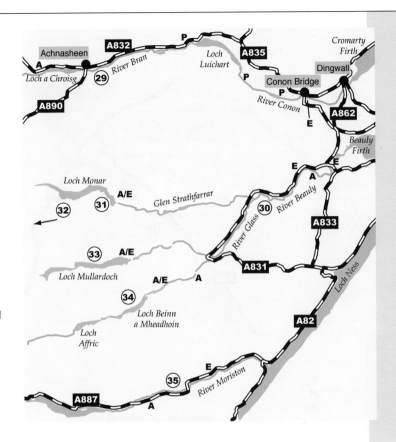

Inverness

029 River Conon and Upper Lochs 49
030 River Glass and River Beauly 50
031 Loch Monar 52
032 Loch Monar West to the Sea . 53
033 Loch Mullardoch 54
034 Loch Affric and Loch Beinn a
     Mheadhoin. 54
035 River Moriston 55

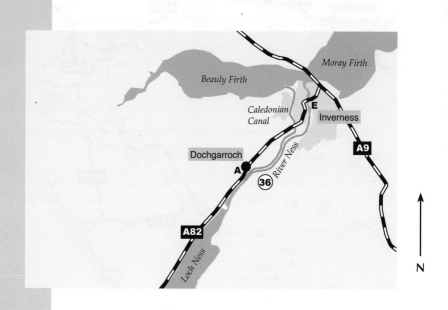

Inverness - continued

036 Loch Ness and River Ness . . 56

Inverness

Inverness is now a city, and a very fast-expanding centre for the north of Scotland. It is essentially an urban centre, but useful for shopping, and has backpacker accommodation, as well as the usual hotels and B&Bs. Several interesting glens come down to Inverness from the west and south.

River Conon and Upper Lochs 029

Portages Two portages of about 2km each.

Introduction An interesting route, taking 2-3 days because of the portages. This route takes the paddler down from Achnasheen on the A832, east to Conon Bridge near Dingwall on the Cromarty Firth. Rough camping available nearly everywhere.

Water Level The River Bran needs to be inspected from the A832 to determine its level… it is usually deep enough.

Access The A832 runs alongside Loch a Chroisg (102586), and also much of the rest of the route.

Campsites & accommodation An expedition involving wild campsites, virtually nothing else on the route.

LENGTH **53km**
OS **25/20/26**
GRADE **1-2**

Description

Km

0   Western end of Loch a Chroisg, west of Achnasheen.
      A832 along north side.

4.5   River Bran leaves eastern end of loch.

5.5   Road bridge, Achnasheen village, burn joins on right.
      A flat river, down a flattish valley – road and railway on
      north side.

18.5 The very winding river enters Loch Achanalt – exit difficult
      to see, around a left-hand bend.

20   After a railway bridge, Loch a Chulinn. Where it narrows,
      after 2km, portage on to road on left bank. The next 2km
      have a barrage, weirs, and power station.

24   Re-enter water 0.5km before a railway bridge. Loch Luichart then commences.

32.5 End of Loch Luichart – portage out on left bank. Portage is of 2km along road on left bank to the power station below the Lochluichart Dam. (If there is water, you might well see many kayakers trying to commit suicide on the very difficult stretch of the Conon, up to grade 5 here).

34.5 On the river! (Conon).

39   Loch Achonachie.

41   Dam – portage right. The Conon now behaves more like a normal lowland river.

45   Moy Bridge.

49.5 Weir, and a large island. Take left fork of river, and shoot weir extreme left down chicken shoot.

52.5 Road bridge (A862). Conon Bridge village to left. Egress below bridge on right side.

030 River Glass and River Beauly

LENGTH **26km**
OS **26**
GRADE **1-2**

Distances 26km for the major trip, a further 6km possible after a portage.

Portages A portage of 2.5km will be required if the inaccessible part of the lower river is to be by-passed.

Introduction This is a virtually ignored gem of a paddle from the Affric foothills, through lofty cliff amphitheatres with mixed woodland, forest and grassy farmland flats. This is Chisholm country, with the Clan seat at Cromar near the start of the paddle, and their eventual base at Erchlass Castle lower down near Struy. Wildlife abounds, eagles are often seen above, and otters, mink and pine martens.

The river divides neatly into two separate days:

      1. Fasnakyle to Mauld.
      2. Mauld to Aigas.

Water Level The latter half of the trip will always be possible, due to the river becoming a reservoir behind the Aigas Dam, otherwise inspect the upper river from the bridge at Cannich.

Access From the A831, which runs by the side of the river up to Cannich bridge (346314), and the minor Glen Affric road, leaving it at the Fasnakyle Power Station (321294). The egress is at the Aigas Dam (473436), access on again at Kiltarlilty Bridge (498440), and final egress at Lovat Bridge (515450).

Campsites & accommodation Campsite and Youth Hostel at Cannich. Cannich and Tomich have B&Bs , and good meals at Tomich Hotel, Slaters Arms, Cannich, and Cnoc and Glass restaurants in Struy.

Description River is grade 1, 2 on some corners, with trees down in places. It is popular with open canoeists, probably because it offers an intrepid-feeling trip, but is not remote at all. There is a strenuous carry out in the Aigas Gorge egress.

Km

0   Fasnakyle Power Station – parking on broad road verges, below power station. Fast section, good fun.

3   Cannich village, campsite just above bridge, steep and bouldery access/egress at bridge.

3.5 River Cannich joins left. River becomes broad with tree-covered islands, and sandbanks. Lots of nice stopping places, long bends.

6.5 Eskadale. Access down a short track, estate road, from B-road on right bank, grassy river bank. After this point, river becomes faster, with trees in water. Care needed.

7.5 River winds near to road on left bank, the main A831. Some parking places on side of road.

14.5 Mauld Bridge – Struy to left. Easy access.

15   River Farrar joins from left, and the access from Struy bridge on the Farrar (0.5km upstream) is quite popular, but parking is very restricted. Turbulence where Farrar joins. (The Farrar is usually regarded as too shallow, but offers paddling possibilities – this does mean gaining access to gated and locked road up Glen Strathfarrar).

23   Eilean Aigas island. By this time, the paddler will have entered what is in fact a flat reservoir, (about 2km upstream) but not like one you have seen before! The island should be taken on the left side, but it can be circumnavigated, as there is no current.

In low water, slight step in middle of gorge.
On the right side is a fantastic road bridge access to the island, worth seeing. This is the Aigas Gorge, said to have one of the most Wow! factors of any open canoe trip in Scotland.

26   Aigas Power Station and dam. The egress is via a grass track on left side, before the dam, which leads up to a short tarmac road to the dam, from a car park.
The next part of the river is a problem, as there is another dam 2km downstream at Kilmorack, and no physical access. However, for those wishing to split the trip, and continue, the bridge just below Kilmorack offers access.
It appears that the River Glass becomes the Beauly below this point.

28.5   Kiltarlilty bridge. Parking and access on south (right) side. Many fishermen here in good water conditions.

29.5   Cruives Weir, long sloping weir.

34.5   Lovat Bridge, egress on right side, above bridge. River becomes tidal, no further easy access, apart from perhaps a muddy exit at the back of Beauly village on left bank.

031 Loch Monar

LENGTH **26**km
OS   **25**
GRADE   -

Distances 26km round trip.

Introduction Loch Monar has the unfortunate distinction of possessing a metalled road which is gated and locked at night-time. It is a rather bare landscape, with Munros all around it.

Access The road and the area is owned by the local estate, but run by SNH as a nature reserve. The road runs for 22km up Glen Strathfarrar from Struy bridge (402404) to the dam (203393). Camping is very discouraged, as has been canoeing on the loch, now hopefully opening up with the new legislation.
The only way of doing a 'bandit-run' is to take boats in somewhat disguised, but the loch itself has been regularly paddled, canoeists being hardy people.

Campsites & accommodation Cannich.

Description The landscape is rough and barren, the loch as a reservoir having the usual rocky sides in low water. It is 13km long. At least the paddler will see almost no one!

Loch Monar West to the Sea 032

Grade Sections of grade 1, 2 and 3 (some waterfalls).

Portages Probably 7 portages. 4 'uphill' portages, one of 1km, another of 0.5 km, and 3 'downhill', avoiding rapids and waterfalls.

Introduction This is a creative route, only done (at the time of writing) by one person to the author's knowledge (and by kayak). It is very remote and serious, in that it has both rapids and waterfalls on the descent to the sea. Loch Monar is the 'private' and gated access road loch which can be frustrating to paddlers wishing for a longer expedition.
The route reaches the west coast at Loch Long, which runs off Loch Alsh.

Water Level The river sections need to be done after wet weather.

Access From Loch Monar, as in Route 031.

Campsites & accommodation Wilderness route, with rough camping.

Description Paddle along Loch Monar west for 9km to Pait Lodge on the south side in an obvious bay. The route then goes 'uphill' via a short river to An Gead Loch, Loch an Tachdaich, a short burn up to Lochan Gobhlach, and a very short burn to another upper lochan.
This 6km, of not very high gradient, will have brought you to the east/west watershed, at a very obvious and wet bog. The headwaters of the River Ling are only 0.5km to the south-west. An initial 1.5km of the Allt an Loin-fhioda starts a westerly descent, to Loch Cruoshie, then 3.5km of flat river, followed by 2.5km of rapids down to the junction with the Blackwater, forming the River Ling.
The river falls rapidly over the next 3km until it is joined by a large burn from the south-east. The Ling then slows down and

LENGTH	**36km**
OS	**25/33**
GRADE	**1/2/3**

flattens for 5km until it enters a final gorge containing two large waterfalls. There is a footpath on the right bank here, and a 4x4 road high on the left bank. After 2km of gorge, a very final 1km leads into Loch Long, and a road of 9km down to Dornie.

Other important points The route is 36km long, and takes 2-3 days.

033 Loch Mullardoch

LENGTH **26km**
OS   **25**
GRADE   -

Distances 26km round trip.

Introduction Loch Mullardoch is a long reservoir, which has banks drying out in low water.

Access Here at least the road is public, the minor road following the River Cannich up from the A831 in Strathglass (338319) to the dam (220317).

Campsites & accommodation At Cannich. The area of the loch is wilderness.

Description The loch is a 13km long reservoir, and 'boating' has been discouraged in the past. Again, Munros dominate to both north and south.

Other important points Interestingly, at the west end it is only 3.5km to the east-west watershed, and a further 13km down to the tidal limit on a small river entering Loch Long. Has anyone paddled this?

034 Loch Affric And Loch Beinn a Mheadhoin

LENGTH **30km**
OS   **25**
GRADE   -

Distances 30km round trip.

Introduction Glen Affric is worth visiting in its own right, a glen which is being replanted by 'Trees for Scotland', but it also offers two lochs set in beautiful scenery.

Access The road runs up Strathglass from Inverness to Cannich, and then a minor road heads up the glen to a dead end near to the top end of Loch Beinn a Mheadhoin at a parking place (216242).

Campsites & accommodation Cannich.

Description Loch Beinn a Mheadhoin can be accessed from near to the dam, where the River Affric leaves. The loch is 9km long, heavily wooded, with inlets and islands. At the top of this loch is a short 'uphill' to Loch Affric, a 100m river. A further 6km will bring you to the top of the loch, in one of Scotland's great wildernesses, famous with climbers and walkers. Glen Affric is the site of one of Scotland's greatest forest regeneration schemes.

River Moriston   035

Introduction A tranquil, lovely river, not often paddled, either because the glen is a bit further to travel to, or because of its only association with the white water stretch below Dundreggan Reservoir, which flows into Loch Ness at Invermoriston.

LENGTH	**14**km
OS	**34**
GRADE	**1/2**

Water Level The level is easy to judge at the put-in, below which are some easy grade 1 rapids - too rocky and 'scrapey', and the river is too low. In flood, the river is a more serious proposition.

Access Glen Moriston is the route of Bonnie Prince Charlie's flight to Glen Elg and Skye. The put in, at Mackenzie's grave, is where Roderick Mackenzie is said to have deliberately sacrificed himself to the Redcoats, as a 'doppleganger', or substitute, in order to give the real prince time to escape. A roadside cairn, consecrated grave and memorial mark the spot, and this is about 3km down the river on the A887 (237112), the main east-west road, from its junction with the A87 from Invergarry.
Egress is on the left side, well before the dam, (351154), just where the forestry meets the main road, and an Armco barrier finishes. An old track runs up to the road. After this, the sides become steeper and rocky.

Campsites & accommodation Nearest proper campsites are down on Loch Ness side, or at Fort Augustus. Invermoriston village has B&Bs, a restaurant and a hotel. In the summer at the village hall, as in many Highland communities, there are light lunches, and toilets available.

Description The glen is broad and well-farmed, virtually no habitation on the river, and very much quieter than the trunk road above would suggest. Ospreys are seen in the glen, at this their northern margin of range in Scotland.

Km

0   Mackenzie's Grave. Lay-by and steps down. Good current, eddy upstream.
        Islands, wooded banks, and plenty of stopping places.

9   Torgoyle bridge, main road passes over. Bridge built by Thomas Telford in 1808, swept away by a flood in 1818, and rebuilt in 1828. Almost identical design to Telford's bridge over the Tay at Dunkeld.

11   River becomes bouldery and braided, faster water.

12.5   River slows down as it imperceptibly becomes the reservoir behind Dundreggan Dam.

14   Egress is on the left side, well before the dam (351154), just where the forestry meets the main road, and an Armco barrier finishes. An old track runs up to the road. After this, the sides become steeper and rocky.

036 Loch Ness and River Ness

LEN. **39.5km**
OS   **26**
GRADE   **1-2**

Distances Loch Ness - 38km, River Ness - 11.5km.

Introduction The Ness is the outlet for Loch Ness, and at some times of year flows fast and powerfully with such a massive amount of water behind it. A trip from the top of the river also offers access to the north end of the loch, with endless kilometres of paddling. The river is pleasant and rural, considering the nearness of Inverness. Bird life is plentiful.

Water Level The River Ness is reached at Dochfour Weir, some rocks showing indicates a medium level. If covered, the river is high. If the rapids and weirs are a bit too much in flood, they can all be portaged.

Access From Dochgarroch on the A82 south of Inverness (618405), giving access on to the Caledonian Canal, which can be paddled south to reach the river, or to go on Loch Ness. Egress at Bught Park in Inverness (664440).

Campsites & accommodation At Dochgarroch.

Description

Km

0   Dochgarroch, 7km out of Inverness. Launch at/near the campsite, and paddle up the canal to reach the river at a weir. The alternative is to go 3km upstream to Lochend, above the extension to Loch Ness, Loch Dochfour. Dochfour Weir is the first weir, usually shot down main chute. If too low, boats can be carried over face of weir, which will be grassy. Islands, rapids and waves.

2.5 Broken weir, with waves.

5.5 Holm Mills Weir. Shoot extreme right, avoid sluice gates. Main chute might be possible, but inspect for rocks. Gentle rapids after this into Inverness.

7.5 Islands – Bught Park to left, parking and egress. It is possible to proceed downriver, but through the town, the river runs fast, with little easy egress, or parking for vehicles.

11.5 South Kessock on left bank – egress, but not good scenery.

13   North Kessock, on north side of Beauly Firth, with parking and egress (only recommended in calm weather).

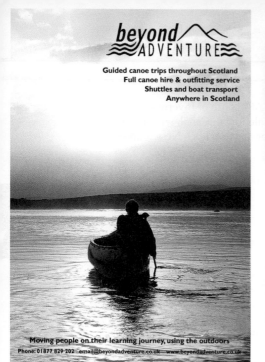

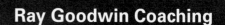

West

West

Kyle of Lochalsh

037 Crowlin Islands 61
038 Loch Kishorn and Loch Carron. 61
039 Loch Duich, Loch Alsh and
     Loch Long 62
040 Loch Duich to Loch Hourn . . . 63
041 Loch Hourn 64

Mallaig

042 Loch Nevis. 66
043 Loch Morar 66
044 Loch Morar and Loch Nevis. . . 67
045 Loch Shiel 68
046 Loch Shiel, River Shiel,
     Loch Moidart and Loch Eilt . . . 73
047 Loch Moidart 74
048 Loch Sunart 75

Fort William

049 Loch Quoich, Upper River Garry
     and Loch Garry 80
050 Loch Oich and Loch Lochy . . . 81
051 Loch Arkaig 81
052 River Lochy 82
053 Loch Laggan and Loch Spean. . 83
054 Loch Treig 84
055 Loch Linnhe. 85
056 Loch Leven 85
057 Rannoch Moor – Lochs Bà and
     Laidon, Rannoch Station 86
058 Loch Creran 87

Oban

059 Loch Etive 90
060 Lower Orchy 91
061 Loch Awe. 92
062 Loch Avich. 93
063 Loch Melfort and Nearby Islands. 94

Lochgilphead

064 Loch Craignish. 96
065 River Add and Loch Crinan . . . 97
066 Crinan Canal 97
067 Tayvallich and Loch Sween . . . 98
068 West Loch Tarbert 99

Cowal

069 Loch Fyne 102
070 Isle of Bute and Nearby Lochs 103
071 Lochs Long, Goil, Holy Loch
     and Gare Loch 104
072 Loch Lomond. 109
073 Loch Lomond, River Leven, Firth
     of Clyde and Loch Long 111
074 Endrick Water 112

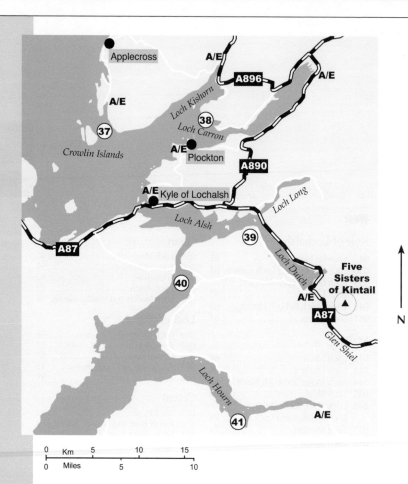

Kyle of Lochalsh

037 Crowlin Islands 61
038 Loch Kishorn and Loch Carron 61
039 Loch Duich, Loch Alsh and
     Loch Long 62
040 Loch Duich to Loch Hourn. . 63
041 Loch Hourn 64

Kyle of Lochalsh

This area is the gateway to Skye, with many walking, climbing and canoeing opportunities. Lochalsh is the main village. The lochs to the north are fairly isolated, as is the Applecross peninsula.

Crowlin Islands 037

Introduction A trip across open sea to some interesting islands.

Access These islands provide a nice little trip in very settled weather, from Toscaig at the very end of the public road (710378).

Campsites & accommodation There is camping at Applecross, 7km north.

Description The islands are 3km from the mainland, the last 1km being exposed. There are three islands, with 'The Harbour' being the very narrow strait between the two largest islands, but fine for canoes and kayaks – the gap is filled with water at high tide. Eilean Mor, the largest island, used to be inhabited and has ruined houses on the east side.

LENGTH	6km
OS	24
GRADE	-

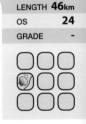

Loch Kishorn and Loch Carron 038

Distances Round trip of 46km from Plockton.

Introduction These two connected lochs provide a paddle in fairly sheltered water, with magnificent mountain views. The main attraction in the area is Plockton village, of Hamish Macbeth TV fame, in Loch Carron.

Access From Plockton (8034), at the end of a minor road from Kyle of Lochalsh; from Lochcarron (8939) on the A896 from Dingwall; and Ardarroch (833400), further west from Lochcarron on the A896.

Campsites & accommodation Balmacara, just east of Kyle of Lochalsh.

Description Loch Kishorn, which used to have oil platform building operations, has 3.5km between Kishorn Island at its mouth,

LENGTH	46km
OS	24
GRADE	-

and Ardarroch village at its head. It is 4.5km from Kishorn Island over to Plockton village, in Loch Carron. The route has islands and buoys, and Plockton is a very sheltered anchorage, and very popular with yachtsmen in the summer. It is also very mild, with many palm trees. Travel E/NE for 15km to the very shallow and muddy head of the loch, passing the narrows at Stromeferry (former ferry point), and Lochcarron village, where the A896 road joins the loch. This is now in the heart of the Wester Ross mountains.
Glencarron has a river, the Carron, which could be paddled the last few kilometres down the glen, but it finishes in the very muddy estuary at low tide.

039 Loch Duich, Loch Alsh and Loch Long

LENGTH **63km**

OS   **33/25**

GRADE   -

Distances Round trip of 63km from Kyle.

Introduction These three lochs stretch inland from Skye and the Kyle, and again provide safe paddling in mouth-watering scenery. The outer part of Loch Alsh has strong tides, as sea water pours through Kyle Rhea to the south. The rest of the lochs have only weak tides.

Access From the A87 along the north side of both Loch Duich and Loch Alsh.

Campsites & accommodation Balmacara and Glenshiel.

Description At Kyleakin, there is much ship traffic proceeding either north or south under the Skye Bridge (always a good photo opportunity), and passage east from here (7627) close to the north shore is advised. Camping at Balmacara (802280) just 4km east of Lochalsh. The coast is low and rocky, 5km from Balmacara to Glas Eilean, then 3km on to Dornie village (shops, B&Bs etc).
From here, Loch Long extends 11km to the north-east, in a very narrow and interesting fjord-like valley between mountains. Also at Dornie is the famous Eilean Donan castle on its rock promontary, one of the most photographed castles in Scotland, if not Europe – well worth visiting. Loch Duich then runs south-east from this point 8.5km to Shiel Bridge, at the foot of Glenshiel (small campsite here).

Loch Duich to Loch Hourn 040

Introduction See sections on Lochs Duich, Alsh and Hourn. This trip is 38km from Shiel Bridge round to Arnisdale on Loch Hourn, another 14km into Kinloch Hourn, the ideal being to take 3 days or so to enjoy the scenery and wildlife.

LENGTH **52km**

OS **33**

GRADE -

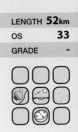

Access Shiel Bridge on A87 (9318), Arnisdale (8410) on Loch Hourn (minor road from Glenelg), and Kinloch Hourn (0695) at head of Loch Hourn, reached by a long single-track road from Invergarry on the Great Glen.

Campsites & accommodation There is a formal site at Shiel Bridge and a bothy and campsite at Barrisdale Bay on Loch Hourn. There is also rough camping.

Description The route is sheltered along the south shore of Lochs Duich and Alsh, but after rounding Garbhan Cosach, Kyle Rhea presents very fast tides, and accurate calculations are necessary. The ideal, no matter how many days are being taken, is to use the ebb tide to take you down Kyle Rhea (7 knots at spring tides!), and on to the area of the Sandaig Islands, or south of here. A flood can then propel you up Loch Hourn. Past the Kyle Rhea ferry is Glenelg, a useful stopping point, with village, shop and pub. Sandaig is the area of 'Ring of Bright Water' country, where the book was written, and this is a region where otters are seen frequently.
The map or chart will tell the paddler that the 4km from Sandaig to Glas Eilean are exposed. 5km from here to the safety and shelter of Arnisdale. Wild campsites are frequent, and of high quality.
For detailed description of the end of the trip, see Route 041 Loch Hourn.

041 Loch Hourn

LENGTH	**27**km
OS	**33**
GRADE	-

Distances Round trip of 27km.

Introduction Loch Hourn is one of the magnificent west coast fjords giving access to Knoydart, and well worth a trip in its own right.

Access At the head of Loch Hourn is Kinlochhourn (0695), now with a sensible car park, where vehicles may be left for days. The access road from Glen Garry and Glen Quoich is very narrow and steep, with many awkward corners. There are no other roads out to Knoydart, only a track for walkers out to Barrisdale Bay (8604).

Campsites & accommodation Plenty of rough camping out on Knoydart, with a bothy and campsite at Barrisdale Bay.

Description The first part out into the loch is narrow, with swift tides, and after 5.5km the narrows at Caolas Mor is reached. Progress will not be made against the tide here. A further 2km brings you round to the beautiful Barrisdale Bay to the left (south), which offers a campsite at Barrisdale Farm, and access to the Knoydart mountains. The most sensible plan is to calculate to arrive at the narrows just before high tide, and in the bay at high tide, to avoid a long portage ashore.
A 6km paddle further out to the north shore reaches Arnisdale, from where a ferry runs to Barrisdale in the summer. A further 5km brings one to the headland on the south side, but there is a lot of exposure here.

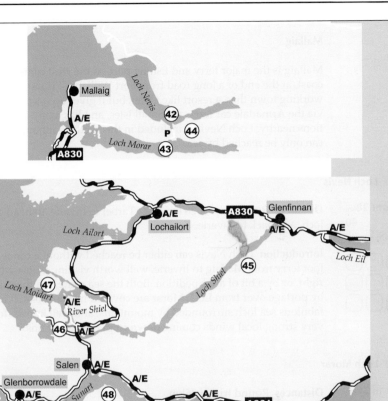

Mallaig

042 Loch Nevis 66
043 Loch Morar 66
044 Loch Morar and Loch Nevis . 67
045 Loch Shiel 68
046 Loch Shiel, River Shiel,
    Loch Moidart and Loch Eilt . . 73
047 Loch Moidart 74
048 Loch Sunart 75

Mallaig

Mallaig is the major ferry and fishing port on the west central coast, at the end of a long road from Fort William. It is more a working town than a resort like Oban, but it gives access to Skye via the Armadale car ferry, the Small Isles, and has many attractions nearby. Loch Nevis is included in this section, although it can only be reached by sea.

042 Loch Nevis

LENGTH **28**km	
OS	**40**
GRADE	-

Distances Round trip of 28 km from Tarbet to Inverie, to head of loch, and back to Inverie.

Introduction Loch Nevis can either be reached without a canoe by foot ferry from Mallaig to Inverie, well worth visiting in its own right, or by a bit of an expedition. Both the sea route and the route by portage over from Loch Morar are covered in Route 044. It is a fabulous sea loch surrounded by mountains, and well known for very strong local winds coming down from the mountains.

043 Loch Morar

LENGTH **36**km	
OS	**40**
GRADE	-

Distances Round trip of 36km.

Introduction A lovely west coast loch, separated from the sea by the sands of the very short River Morar, and the main road to Mallaig. It is obviously more sheltered than the sea lochs to the north.

Access Loch Morar is easily accessed from Mallaig and Arisaig, a minor road leading off the A830 to a pier alongside the first part of the loch (689929), and eventually to the hamlet of Bracorina. In the past, before the new Land Reform Act, access was either barred here, or payment requested.

Campsites & accommodation The nearest formal sites are just south towards Arisaig (6 sites at the last count, some of which may only take caravans, on this lovely stretch of coast). Plenty of rough sites along Loch Morar.

Description There are attractive wooded islands in the first few km, and the loch stretches some 18km to the east, being a uniform 2km wide, narrowing to 1km. After 10km paddling east, there is a pier on the south side giving access to an estate, and after 11km, on the north side is the landing and portage at Swordland (or just round the corner at South Tarbet bay), over to Loch Nevis at Tarbet. (See Route 044). A further 7km to the end of the loch leads to Glen Pean and Glen Dessary, great walking country.

Loch Morar and Loch Nevis 044

Distances Possible expeditions of 40 km round trip, either using the route to reach Inverie, or the head of Loch Nevis. Round trip of 26km to reach Mallaig.

LENGTH **40**km

OS   **33/40**

GRADE   -

Portages One portage of 2km over the tarbet between the two lochs.

Introduction A fine trip in great scenery, which can be quite safe if conditions are closely observed on Loch Nevis. A week's holiday can be spent in this area.

Access From the pier on Loch Morar (689929).

Campsites & accommodation Rough camping.

Description The classic way into Loch Nevis is by Loch Morar, along to Swordland, and then over the portage to Tarbet, a not too rough way (track with stones) over the pass, just under 2km. On the north side is a chapel converted into a bothy, and camping available. There are two great directions to go now: east, up Loch Nevis to the head, 8km, or west 8km, out to Inverie, the 'capital village' of Knoydart, with its pub and lively social scene. To do both will usually take 4 days, with start and return to the west end of Loch Morar. A different route, with more risk, is to return by sea to Mallaig, which is 9.5km. The safest way is to cross over (away from the ferry and fishing boat route) to the south shore off Sgeir a Ghaill, sheltered from westerlies, and then hug the south shore, which is high and rocky. This trip is only about 2 hours max with the tide, so the risk is quite slight, if prevailing weather is benign. Whichever way you go, this is a west coast classic.

045 Loch Shiel

LENGTH **60km**
OS **40**
GRADE -

Distances Round trip of 60km.

Introduction Mention is made here of Loch Shiel for the casual visitor, but the area is far better known as both a longer expedition, and a unique 'round trip', detailed in Route 046. It is probably the second-most frequent canoe trip undertaken in Scotland. The loch is a wilderness experience, no roads leading into most of its banks, and is 30km long from Glenfinnan, the famous monument on the 'Road to the Isles' at the north end, to Acharacle at the southern end. Wildlife is plentiful, with otters, pine marten, golden eagle, and if very lucky, wild cats.

Access Access may be had at the north end, Glenfinnan, via the hotel (a fishing pier just down the loch being made unavailable in 2003) (901805). At Acharacle, access/egress can be slightly difficult. A pier on the left (east) side at Acharacle is much used by commercial boats, and there is almost no parking. A better bet is to egress just after the bridge, entering the River Shiel on the left bank. All the roads in the area are narrow, with little parking.

Campsites & accommodation Rough camping in many places down the loch. In summer, shingle spits are better to avoid midges. In the general area, the formal site at Resipole on Loch Sunart is the nearest.

Description The scenery is superb all the way down. A day trip will only take the paddler halfway down and back, but camping can be had in many places. Small islands become much more frequent about halfway down. After 20km is the first large bay on the left, where the River Polloch comes in, with Polloch village 1km inland from the end of the inlet, with a road egress (a very tortuous road over from Strontian on Loch Sunart).
2km further on at the narrows is the well-known Burial Ground Island, Eilean Fhianain, and St. Firman's Chapel. The left bank then opens out into Claish Moss, a large bog, and Acharacle follows after a further 6km.

Improvised sail on Loch Lochy - www.RayGoodwin.com

Mallaig to Loch Nevis in the perfect conditions required - www.RayGoodwin.com

Upper Loch Nevis - www.RayGoodwin.com

Portage to Loch Nevis -

Loch Shiel, River Shiel, Loch Moidart and Loch Eilt 046

Distances Glenfinnan, start and finish, 70km. Fort William, start and finish, 110km.

LENGTH **70**km
OS **40/41**
GRADE **1/2**

Grade Grade 1 and 2, although the fall at the end of the River Shiel might be more difficult (subject to tide).

Portages The Glenfinnan circuit has portages of 2.5km up the River Ailort, and 6km from Loch Eilt to Loch Shiel.
The Fort William circuit has, in addition to the two portages above, one of 6km each way between Loch Shiel and Loch Eil.

Introduction This trip of 4 days or so duration is a Scottish classic, and has been extended to a longer expedition leaving Fort William, and using Loch Eil and its connecting rivers to Glenfinnan. It is popular because it is circular, one of few in Scotland using rivers and lochs, and because of the scenery of Loch Shiel and the coast.

Water Level The River Shiel can be very shallow in summer, the height is obvious from Shiel Bridge, Acharacle.

Access At Glenfinnan, hotel pier (901805), egress possible at Acharacle (southern end of Loch Shiel), A860 at Glenuig (674777), A861 alongside Loch Ailort (various places over 4km), Lochailort village (768824), and Glenfinnan.

Campsites & accommodation Plenty of rough sites. The nearest formal site is at Resipole, Loch Sunart (not on route).

Description See Route 045 Loch Shiel, and Route 047 Loch Moidart. The River Shiel (only 3.5km long) has had 'awkward' anglers in the past, especially at the bottom, where a sizeable rapid debouches you into the sea at low tide. The river is narrow all the way down, with fishing platforms and other detritus sticking out into the channel – no other obstacles. Leaving Moidart by North Channel, turn north for 5km of coast, with pleasant islands and inlets inside of Samalaman Island, to Glenuig, a very hospitable place, with a famous village hall offering great music all through the summer. Camping on the foreshore here.
3.5km on to Roshven, and then 2 more km to islands, often used for camping. The scenery remains fine, and it is only 5km more to

Lochailort village. Then 2.5km portage to Loch Eilt, 5.5km long, and 7km portage on to Glenfinnan (or leave a car at Lochailort!).

047 Loch Moidart

LENGTH **22km**
OS   **40**
GRADE   -

Distances Round trip of 22km.

Introduction Loch Moidart is also part of the classic circular journey in Route 046, but worth visiting in its own right.

Access The head at Ardmorlich pier on the A861 (697728) is often dry, and a more reliable way of finding water is to travel down to Castle Tioram (663724), a ruin reached down the road running alongside the River Shiel from Shiel Bridge. There is a car park at the end, much used by walkers, and people who come to stare at the castle, crumbling away due to arguments between its owner and the conservation authorities.

Campsites & accommodation There are great campsites all over this area, especially on islands. Keep away from houses.

Description Launching will always be possible at Castle Tioram (pronounced 'Churram)'), and the paddler has then the glories of Shona Beag and Eilean Shona islands, as well as a couple of smaller islands to paddle around (14km for the round trip). If feeling brave, there is a little expedition to the south well worth carrying out, to go out of South Channel, and turn left at Farquhar's Point, some 2.5km round to Ardtoe (628708), a delightful spot with beautiful sandy beaches. Inland from here is Kentra, an interesting area of little creeks, if there is water. Then 2.5km further south-west from Ardtoe is Gortenfern (612691), with another fabulous beach, also reached by a walk from Arivegaig.

Loch Sunart 048

LENGTH	**38km**
OS	**40/49**
GRADE	-

Distances Round trip of 38km.

Introduction Loch Sunart is another fabulous area, easily pro-viding a week's holiday with different trips each day. A base at, say, Resipole campsite just before Salen, gives access to beaches on Ardnamurchan, the whole of the main loch, Loch Shiel to the north, and Loch Teacuis on the south side, an area few people are privileged to see, especially by water. The OS maps above do not cover the first seaward end of Loch Sunart, but this area is unlikely to attract, being open to the sea from the west.

Access The north side has a road all the way along it, the A861 as far as Salen, and then the B8007 which eventually winds its way to Ardnamurchan Point. Access may be had at Strontian (815615), Resipole Farm and landing (725640), Salen (690648), a useful picnic and car park near to the west (680630) and, with some dif-ficulty, near to the Glenborrodale Hotel (620606). However all of the roads are narrow, mostly single-track, and can be extremely congested in summer. Care is especially required with trailers.

Campsites & accommodation Resipole campsite is well-situated, with space for tents, caravans, and camper vans, and it has cabins for rent, as well as a bar and restaurant. There is no other site in the area.

Description Due to the normal prevailing tide and wind further out in the loch, it is advised to access from the Ardnamurchan road, around Glenborrodale, north side (actually little parking in this area, hotel just east of Glenborrodale has a jetty and will prob-ably oblige).
Isle of Risga lies just off here, and a passage east, using the shelter, can mean a crossing over to Carna, west side if weather fair, and entering Loch Teacuis through the very narrow western passage. The tide runs very fast here, enter preferably at near top of flood. The loch is 5km long, and very wild and isolated. There are camp-sites, but also terrible midges in summer. East passage is wider, but with two rock reefs, an interesting paddle or sail.
Carna to Salen village, 9km. There is a picnic site on the left bank, just before Salen, which is extremely convenient for launching.

Resipole campsite is 3.5km further on. The Ben Resipole path leaves from the campsite.

Opposite Resipole are some small islets, lots of seals.

Resipole to the 'Narrows', Glas Eilean, 5km. Nice islands on left side, habitat for otters. The narrow part has, as expected, strong tides.

Glas Eilean to Strontian village, 6km. At low tide, much mud and sand off Strontian. There is a jetty 1km further on which is easier, with parking. Strontian is the main centre up at this part of the loch, but don't expect supermarkets!

The parking of vehicles is difficult in the whole of this area; the roads are narrow with passing places only in most places.

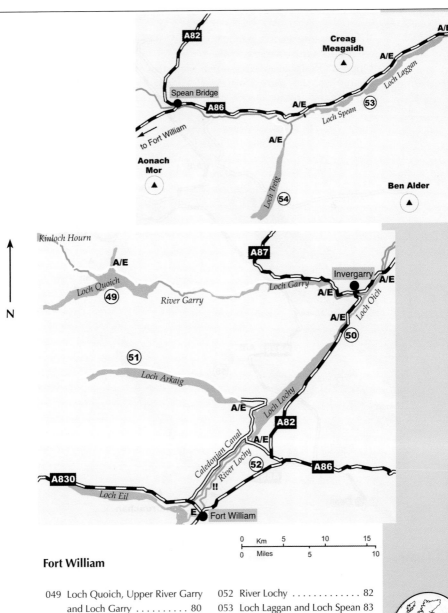

Fort William

049 Loch Quoich, Upper River Garry
     and Loch Garry 80
050 Loch Oich and Loch Lochy. . 81
051 Loch Arkaig 81
052 River Lochy 82
053 Loch Laggan and Loch Spean 83
054 Loch Treig. 84

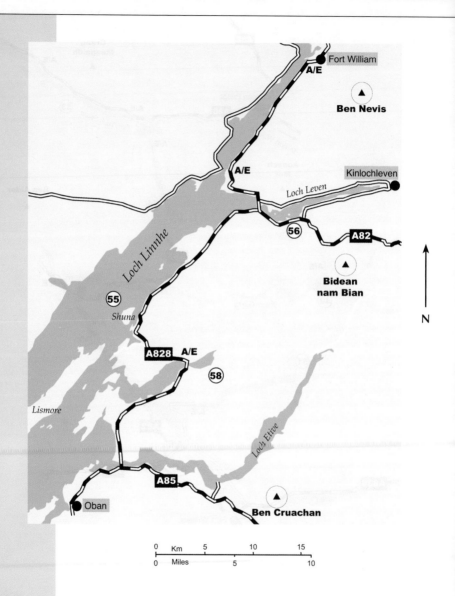

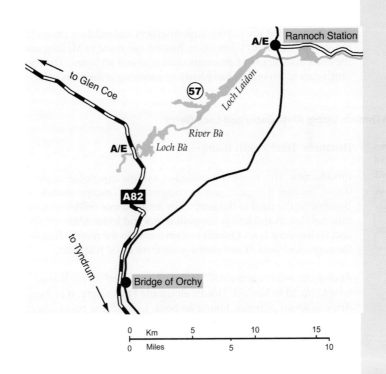

Fort William - continued

055 Loch Linnhe 85
056 Loch Leven. 85
057 Rannoch Moor - Lochs Bà and
     Laidon, Rannoch Station . . . 86
058 Loch Creran 87

Fort William

Fort William is a famous and obvious centre for outdoor activities in Scotland. It has high mountains, including Ben Nevis, but as one of the wettest places in the UK is also probably the Scottish centre for white water paddling. There are some wet-weather attractions in the town, plus supermarkets and outdoor shops.It is the start of the Great Glen route, has the rail route to Mallaig and the Isles, and plenty of accommodation to suit all tastes. The road north-east to Inverness has plenty of canoeing attractions off it.

049 Loch Quoich, Upper River Garry and Loch Garry

LENGTH **46**km
OS   **33/34**
GRADE   **1/2**

Distances Total length 46km.

Introduction This route is included as a single trip, not an expedition, because it is quite easy to complete, with escape always possible on the road to the north. The area is a true wilderness, with little habitation and lovely unspoilt rivers and lochs. Many climbers and walkers use Loch Quoich to gain access to the many Munros to the south and west. It can give a good three days' paddling.

Access Access is via the A87 to Skye, turning off on the B-road (single track) to Kinloch Hourn alongside Loch Garry. It is then a drive of about 20 miles, taking an hour, to reach the point where the road starts to leave Loch Quoich (989036). If Loch Quoich is low, access should be had wherever the road is near water. From the bridge over an arm of the loch, (015040), it is 10km to the head, in a mountain fastness, unforgettable camping. Egress near to Garry dam (276023).

Campsites & accommodation
Wilderness camping. The site at the western end of the loch, surrounded by high mountains is unforgettable.

Description From the head of the loch, east to the dam is 14km, with a carry over the dam via the road, and 3km on the Geart Garry to join the River Kingie, occasional rapids. At the junction, the river is far bigger and flows around wooded islands imperceptibly into Loch Poulary, which then becomes the River Garry, and

into Loch Garry 8km downstream. There is one large rapid around
islands on this stretch. Great campsites on some of the islands.
Loch Garry is 11km long, passing under an estate bridge at narrows, a third of the way down. Egress is on to a track on left side,
just before the dam. Below the dam is the white water Garry (See
Scottish White Water).

Loch Oich and Loch Lochy 050

Distances Loch Lochy 15km, Canal is 2.5km, and Loch Oich 6km.

LEN.	**23.5**km
OS	34
GRADE	-

Portages Portage at Laggan Locks at north end of Loch Lochy.

Introduction These two lochs provide useful day trips in great
scenery, Loch Lochy being the first experience many paddlers
have of Canadian-like lake scenery.

Access Road access to both lochs is from the main A82 road
which runs up the glen, many parking places on east side of Loch
Lochy (2591 to 2794), fewer on Loch Oich, though there is one
picnic site on west bank (304989).

Campsites & accommodation Wilderness sites on west side of
Loch Lochy, and possibly near to mouth of River Garry, west side
of Loch Oich.

Description Full details in the Cross-Scotland section, Route 129
Great Glen, Fort William to Inverness. Lochy is large, Oich is
small and cosy, with interesting wooded islands.

Loch Arkaig 051

Distances Round trip of 38km.

LENGTH	**38**km
OS	33/34
GRADE	-

Introduction Loch Arkaig is an enormous and hidden loch, usually found by paddlers doing the very short River Arkaig. The
very long and tedious lochside road gives access to the mountains
of Glen Dessary at the west end.

Access The B8005 leaves the Caledonian Canal at Gairlochy, 5km from Spean Bridge, crosses the outlet of the River Arkaig, winds through woodland, and emerges at the bottom end of Loch Arkaig. Parking is very restricted, there being a spot by the waterfalls 0.5km from the east end of the loch, (176889) and some space right on the loch at its foot (172888).

Campsites & accommodation The only spaces for rough camping appear to be right at the west end of the road alongside the loch.

Description There is no habitation to speak of and the loch is 19km long, an almost uniform 1km wide. The upper reaches are amongst one of the wildest parts of Scotland, Knoydart lying to the west of here.

The braver might want to paddle the river out, which is quite easy apart from the one grade 4 rapid (see Scottish White Water). The very short 2km river spits out the paddler very suddenly, onto the stillness of Loch Lochy at Bunarkaig, with a 4km trip south to either Gairlochy lock on the canal, or onto the River Lochy.

052 River Lochy

LEN. **11.5km**
OS **41**
GRADE **1(2-3)**

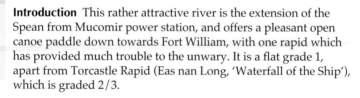

Grade Grade 1, apart from Torcastle Rapid, grade 2-3, which can be portaged on the right-hand side over rocks.

Introduction This rather attractive river is the extension of the Spean from Mucomir power station, and offers a pleasant open canoe paddle down towards Fort William, with one rapid which has provided much trouble to the unwary. It is a flat grade 1, apart from Torcastle Rapid (Eas nan Long, 'Waterfall of the Ship'), which is graded 2/3.

Water Level The first shingle rapids downstream of the start are a good indication of level.

Access From the B8004, after it passes Mucomir power station, north-west of Spean Bridge (183839). Egress on to left bank, just above outflow from Fort William smelter, just after railway bridge (119755). To reach this by road, drive towards Fort William on the A82, and half a mile after the traffic lights at A830 junction, turn right on to minor road signed Inverlochy Castle. Take first right, then left and park just through the railway bridge.

Campsites & accommodation Torness, near the start, Spean Bridge, or Glen Nevis.

Description

Km

0   Access near Gairlochy, where road leaves the river.

4   River Loy (see Scottish White Water) joins on right. It is worth a walk to see where the Loy flows under the Caledonian Canal aqueduct, and it can be paddled with water.

7   Torcastle Rapid is heralded by the river flowing left through a gap, and a change to a rocky river bed. The river drops between rock walls. In low water, it is a drop on the right into a pool; in high flows, the water is more confused and boily. Many capsizes here! Rescue however is easy, as is taking photos from the right bank. Rocks and trees in water follow. River then slows down and meanders.

9.5 On a long, long left-hand bend, egress is possible on to right bank, just after houses.

11   Main road bridge, Fort William to Mallaig road.

11.5 Railway bridge follows, and then egress can be made on to a lane from the main road. At the egress is also outflow from aluminimum works, which can offer sport to headbangers.

Loch Laggan and Loch Spean 053

Introduction These two lochs are linked, and often regarded as one piece of water. They were formed when British Aluminium dammed up the Spean, and then diverted the headwaters of the Spey from the north into the same system. The scenery around Loch Laggan is familiar to many TV viewers, due to the popularity of 'Monarch of the Glen', filmed around here.
The reservoirs can be quite empty in dry periods.

LENGTH **17**km

OS   **41/42**

GRADE   -

Access Access can be had at the eastern end at Kinloch Laggan, on the River Pattack, off the A86, main east-west road (538898). Access/egress also from where the river coming down the Creag Meagaidh corrie joins the loch, where there is also a good car park (481870). Final egress off at the dam (371809) where there is some parking.

Campsites & accommodation Roybridge, Inverroy and Spean Bridge. Bunkhouse at Roybridge.

Description It is 11km to the western end, with an attractive sandy beach at the eastern end when dry. Ardverikie Castle is very obvious on the south side after a few km, and Munros dominate to both north and south. Halfway down on the north side is the car park for Creag Meagaidh, a good stopping point, and adequate car parking.

The Spean between the two lochs is hardly visible or flowing in high water, when there is one continuous loch. Loch Spean is much smaller and narrower, and visibility is limited of the surroundings due to islands of mud when low. The loch is 5.5km long, with take-out on the north side by the Laggan Dam. If lucky, you might see pipes 'blowing' from this dam, a great sight indeed. It is interesting to go and look at the horrendous gorges lower down the Spean, some drops of which have not been paddled yet.

054 Loch Treig

LENGTH **18km**	
OS	**41**
GRADE	**-**

Distances Round trip of 18km.

Introduction Loch Treig is in a very spectacular position, and usually only seen by passengers on the train from Glasgow, being totally land-locked. It is a reservoir, part of the Glen Spean system, lying south of the main glen, in the Grey Corries set of mountains.

Access Road access is from the minor road to Fersit (353781) off the A86, and at which end is car parking. Up to the date of the Land Reform Act, paddlers had been chased off and threatened.

Campsites & accommodation At Spean Bridge, Inverroy and Roybridge. Bunkhouse at Roybridge.

Description A loch that is 9km long, situated amongst high and wild mountains. There is a hunting lodge at the bottom end, reached only from Corrour Station.

Loch Linnhe 055

Distances Loch Linnhe runs for 50km from Oban north-east to Fort William.

LENGTH **50km**

OS **41/49**

GRADE -

Introduction Loch Linnhe is large and exposed, but a couple of arms off it are included below. It is the main approach for shipping heading for the Caledonian Canal.

Access From Oban, Port Appin, Corran and Fort William on the east side. The west side is much more remote, although the road north from Ardgour, on the west side of the Corran Ferry, is pretty and quieter than the east side.

Campsites & accommodation Sites and accommodation at Oban and Fort William, and also at Glencoe and Ballachulish.

Description North of Oban is the entrance to Loch Etive, also described, and then the narrowing of the Lynn of Lorne towards Appin. This area is interesting, with narrows and islands between Port of Appin and Lismore. Around the north side of Lismore are shallows and islands off Port Ramsay. North of this is Shuna, narrow passage to east, and then the headland between Cuil and Kentallan, good camping possibilities.
Around this corner is the entrance east into Loch Leven and Ballachulish, and then to the north the Corran Narrows, very strong tides, and ferry.
The way up to Fort William is much more sheltered from the wind. At the very top is Corpach, and the entrance to the Caledonian Canal. To the left (west), is Loch Eil.

Loch Leven 056

Distances Round trip of 26km.

LENGTH **26km**

OS **41/49**

GRADE -

Introduction Loch Leven often provides a safe and sheltered sea paddle when it is windy elsewhere, with good mountain scenery all the way up to Kinlochleven.

Access There is a launching ramp just after the Ballachulish Bridge (054598), reached by a minor road from North Ballachulish. The end of the loch at Kinlochleven is very dry at low tide,

but there are several places to egress on the north shore on to small vehicle parking places.

Campsites & accommodation At Kinlochleven, Caolasnacon on the south bank, and in Glen Coe on the south shore.

Description It is 13km up to Kinlochleven, a nice half-day paddle, with the scenery of Glen Coe ever-present. There are various access places on both banks where the trip could be shortened. After 3km paddling east is the island of Eilean Munde, the burial place of the Lords of the Isles. At 5km the loch narrows, and at 8.5km are real narrows. It is advisable to reach the head of the loch at high tide, the drying out part being boulders and seaweed. Kinlochleven is the start of a classic cross-Scotland trip.

057 Rannoch Moor – Lochs Bà and Laidon, Rannoch Station

LENGTH **13km**
OS **41/50/42**
GRADE **1**

Portages In low water and dry summers, the first part of the trip could entail some short portages.

Introduction This is another classic trip, Rannoch Moor never being forgotten by anybody who has crossed it, and many forms of transport have been tried, canoe, kayak, lilo, raft, etc.

Access The start is at one of Britain's most remote and windswept points, as the A82 crosses over to Glen Coe. This comes into the expedition category because high summer brings low water, lots of mud and many midges, other seasons often unseasonable snow and sleet showers. Once on the moor, there is literally no escape, it's either onwards… or back. The vehicle shuttle for this is also massive – almost across Scotland! - about 83 miles one-way to Rannoch Station!
The start is on to Loch Bà on the east side, where a small connecting river flows under the road, the only bridge on this road. It is just after a large lochan on the west side (309495). Beware, there is only one lay-by to park in on this bit of road.
Egress is off the Dubh Lochan, north side (417578) after Loch Laidon.

Campsites & accommodation On the route, look for slightly higher ground – everywhere is boggy. No formal sites nearby, apart from down in Glen Coe.

Description The scenery is very flat, albeit surrounded by mountains, and navigation is therefore quite difficult - a GPS comes into its own in this terrain. Loch Bà is some 2.5km long, and heads generally north-east, but has islands, and is quite misleading. There are two places where the loch narrows, the second one heralding a turn of the loch to the right, and the start of the River Bà. The river is often imperceptible in its flow so not obvious, and in certain levels of water, dead-end channels can mislead paddlers. The river winds for 2.5km eventually into Loch Laidon which is obvious! The intrepid voyageur can now perhaps relax a bit, and enjoy the surrounding scenery. The trip should take more than a day to appreciate this piece of wilderness, and the first more comfortable campsites are on the tiny wooded islands in Loch Laidon. This loch is 8km long, with a long arm out to the north-west into yet more wilderness. The route ahead is framed by the mountains of the Rannoch deer forest to the north.

At the end of Loch Laidon (carefully avoiding the outlet south of the Garbh Ghaoir river), is a short half km portage from the little Dubh Lochan up a track to Rannoch Station.

Loch Creran 058

Introduction This is another arm off Loch Linnhe, not incredibly interesting but the upper loch, now above the new road bridge (formerly railway bridge) is quiet.

LEN.	**12.5**km
OS	**49**
GRADE	-

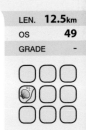

Access From the A828, Oban to Fort William road, on the south side of the new Creagan bridge (976442), or from the minor road to South Shian jetty (909422), off the A828 near Benderloch.

Campsites & accommodation Ledaig, south of Benderloch, or nearer to Oban.

Description The entrance from the sea has very fast tides, being bottle-shaped. Eriska, at the mouth, is a separate island at low tide with a hotel on it. South Shian has a major boatyard and yacht moorings. 10km from the entrance to the A828 bridge, and a further 2.5km to the end.

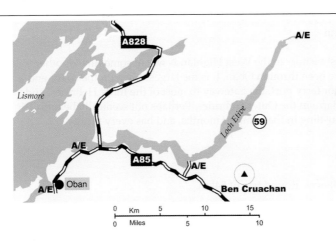

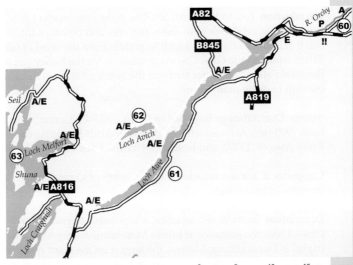

Oban

059 Loch Etive............... 90
060 Lower Orchy 91
061 Loch Awe............... 92
062 Loch Avich 93
063 Loch Melfort and Nearby Islands 94

Oban

Most visitors to the West Highlands will at some time or other
have been through Oban. It is the largest town on the coast, and a
major ferry port, the gateway to most of the Inner Hebrides, and
to Barra in the Outer Hebrides. Perhaps not scenically beautiful, it
is bustling in the summer months, and has every facility.

059 Loch Etive

LENGTH **54km**
OS **49/50**
GRADE -

Distances Round trip of 54km.

Tides The Falls of Lora (tidal falls) provide rough water at certain
states of tide.

Introduction Just to the north of Oban is the entrance to Loch
Etive, a long tidal loch with many features and points of interest. It is mainly known as a loch to paddle from the head at Glen
Etive, amongst the Glen Coe mountains, or for the honey pot of
the tidal Falls of Lora, not far from the entrance and still unusual
enough to draw many tourists.

Access Dunstaffnage Bay, east of Oban (885340); Connel, north
bank (909346); Achnacoich pier (961340); Airds Bay jetty, end of
River Awe (011327); and head of loch from Glen Etive (108450).

Campsites & accommodation Ledaig, north of Connel; rough sites
on sides of upper loch.

Description In sheltered weather, it is possible to paddle up from
Oban. From the entrance at Eilean Mor, immediately to south
(right) is Dunstaffnage Marina, the largest on the coast now, and
after 2km are the Falls of Lora, under Connel Bridge, which run
very strongly on a spring ebb tide. The main passage for boats
is close to the right (south) bank. The left has a rock ledge which
uncovers, and if an ebb tide, there are bound to be small white
water kayaks playing on it. For an easy passage, go up on the
flood.
At 4km, Achnacoich River, fish farms from here on up.
7km, Airds Point. 10km, Bonawe Narrows.
It is a further 17km up to the head, with only mountains, moun-

tains, mountains! Plenty of possible campsites. In the height of summer, the head of the loch can be quite crowded with people camping, so maybe use the advantage of being on the water to avoid this area.

Lower Orchy 060

Portages The portage around the rapids is about 600m long.

LEN.	**12.5**km
OS	**50/55**
GRADE	**(2-3)**

Introduction The Orchy is of course far better known as a white water river, but there is a pleasant stretch where the river flattens out in the lower valley, downstream of the third and final waterfall. There is, however, an unexpected stretch of grade 2-3 rocky rapids in the middle of this part, usually not visited by the kayakers from higher up.
The valley is well known for its wildlife, and you may well see golden eagle and short-eared owl in the daylight, as well as otter.

Access A minor road, the B8074, follows the river most of the way down on its left bank, veering away only when the rapids are coming up. Access below the Falls of Orchy (242320). Egress downstream of the A85 road bridge (138282).

Campsites & accommodation Tyndrum to the east, Bridge of Awe to the west.

Description

Km

0   Eas Urchaidh Falls. Good parking here. If in doubt, inspect the next kilometre of river, as there is a weir just downstream (0.5m drop), with a noticeable towback and some rock ledges.

2   Footbridge, car parking. River flattens out, gravel banks and islands.

6   Grey shed and white house on left bank signals start of rapids. A left and right passage are blocked by boulders. Egress to road on left bank at this point (202285).
      There follows three drops over some 600m. Portage is possible through trees on left bank, but lining down nearly impossible due to trees and rocks. At medium to high water, the rapids are shootable, the only real difficulty being the

high first drop. A rocky approach down left side of an island, leads to an appreciable drop on right side of river, rocky shallows on left. Then a good chute down the left side of next island follows, right side very dry, leading into a final drop on right side of river, which winds back to left of river, and a further 200m of shallow water.

7   At end of rapids, the River Lochy joins from left, good stopping place on right bank.

8.5   After a long quiet stretch, river disappears down a stony chute on right, banks of stones ahead. The chute runs straight into a tree, and traps debris, a common capsize site. Take care.

9.5   Dalmally village bridge. Access on right bank upstream of bridge. Shallows under the bridge.
       The river now becomes braided, with islands and banks of stones. No difficulties. River heads north-west, good views of Ben Cruachan.

11.5   On right bank, as river takes a left-hand bend around an island, sand martin holes in sandy right bank.

12.5   A85(T) road bridge. Paddle down to the railway bridge 200m below, and land immediately under it on the left side, to egress on to a muddy track on the upstream side, another 200m or so from the parking place. (This is a sharp turn off the A85, heading west, just before the road bridge, and is a private access to Kilchurn Castle on Loch Awe).

061 Loch Awe

LENGTH **72km**
OS   **50/55**
GRADE   -

Distances Round trip of 72km.

Introduction The loch is a massive 36km long, and offers a week of paddling with little trouble, especially if Loch Avich and the coast are explored as well. It is very 'Canadian' in appearance, with vast stretches of conifers.

Access There is one problem, namely a frustrating lack of places to access the water, possibly intentional, to prevent those without licences from fishing. This should improve through the good offices of the Forestry Commission, who own virtually all the land around, and have the responsibilities of the Access Code. Access on at top end, below A85 road bridge, off track to Kilchurn Castle (139279); from the B846, on the west side, at North Port (048214); from Dalavich village, on the west side, behind the houses (970126), quite good vehicle parking; and from Ford pier at the bottom end (874045), gate usually locked, but canoes can be carried over, and vehicle parked on a long passing place on the road above.

Campsites & accommodation Bridge of Awe, otherwise rough sites in the forest areas. Once on the water, campsites can be found relatively easily, clearings in the forest being the item to look out for. (You will find the existing small camp and caravan sites are private ones for anglers). The long road down the east side has very few opportunities to access the water, and passing places must not be used for car parking or camping.

Description There are many castles, historic sites, island burial grounds, and crannogs on the loch - go get a map and explore! This is one of the relatively few areas of Scotland where, as a paddler, you will be undisturbed and can paddle for hours or days.

Loch Avich 062

Distances Round trip of 10km.

LENGTH	**10km**
OS	**55**
GRADE	-

Introduction Loch Avich is worth a visit, a small piece of water on the west side, and higher up than Loch Awe.

Access The loch has access from the minor road that runs from Loch Awe to Kilmelford, along its north side. There is a car park (913138) near to a ruined castle on an island.

Campsites & accommodation None local. Asknish bay to the west, on the coast, or Bridge of Awe.

Description Loch Avich is 5km long, with access from the road on the north side. There is a car park near to a ruined castle on an island only a few metres off the mainland, which provides a useful base. The burn coming in at the top can be paddled up a couple of hundred metres. At the lower end is the exit of the River Avich (see Scottish White Water).

063 Loch Melfort and Nearby Islands

LENGTH **40**km
OS   **55**
GRADE   -

Distances Many different trips can be run in this area, of 30-40km circular expeditions.

Introduction The islands of Seil, Luing, Torsa and Shuna are included because this is one of the most sheltered parts of the coastal islands, with plenty of paddling opportunities, if the prevailing weather conditions are taken into account.

Access A base may be had on Seil, either near to 'Atlantic Bridge', (Clachan Bridge 785197), the very narrow channel between the island and mainland, or down at Balvicar Bay (768168). The other possibilities are to launch on Loch Melfort, the head of which is quite dry at low tide, or at Craobh Haven, the marina (795075).

Campsites & accommodation Asknish Bay on the coast, just south of Loch Melfort.

Description Seil is fairly quiet and laid-back, with access south to Cuan Sound, through which the tide rushes, as with all narrow channels in this part of the world. Torsa is just across Cuan Sound, with the delightful Ardinamar Bay to the south.
Seil Sound runs inland of Seil for 8km down to Ardinamar, and it is 8km to the head of Loch Melfort, with a hotel and yacht anchorage and chandlers. The main hive of activity in the area is the newish marina of Craobh Haven, south of Loch Melfort, which was built within three natural islands. The marina has the usual facilities, including a pub with food open all day, a useful service in the area. It is perfectly possible from here to circumnavigate Shuna, in settled sea conditions, and explore the east side of Luing. The western side of both Luing and Seil are very exposed to the weather, and tides run very fast through the Sound of Luing (Fladda).

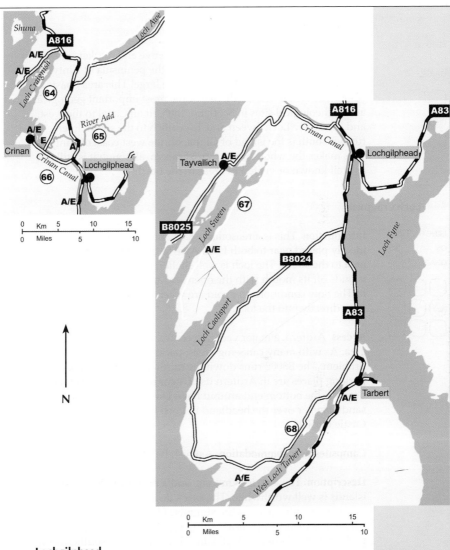

Lochgilphead

064 Loch Craignish 96
065 River Add and Loch Crinan. . 97
066 Crinan Canal 97
067 Tayvallich and Loch Sween . 98
068 West Loch Tarbert. 99

Introduction

This town is tiny, but it is the administrative and market centre for a large area, including the whole of the peninsula of Kintyre. In this part of Scotland, all distances are large! This area boasts Kilmartin Glen to the north, one of the most important geological and archeological sites in Scotland, the Crinan Canal to the west, and the lovely Loch Sween and Tayvallich to the south. Even further south is the island of Gigha, off the west coast of Kintyre. This makes the whole area a tourist mecca, although it is still not as well known or visited as areas to the north.

064 Loch Craignish

LENGTH **12km**

OS   **55**

GRADE   -

Introduction This is a reasonably safe and interesting sea loch, ideally placed near to both Loch Awe to the east, and the Crinan area to the south. The loch is well sheltered from the west, has islands off its mouth with the open sea, and also islands within it. The only conditions to avoid are when a south-westerly swell runs directly into the loch.

Access Ardfern, a major yachting centre, is the main inhabited area. As with many canoeing areas, parking of vehicles can be a problem. The B8002 runs down the northern shore, but the only parking places are in Ardfern itself, near to the hotel (804041), down at the bottom end around Bagh Dun Mhullig (778019), a sandy bay, or over the headland in Loch Beag around Craignish Castle (765006).

Campsites & accommodation Asknish Bay to the north.

Description The loch is 6km long, and a round trip between the islands is well worthwhile. The east side is much quieter than the west, busy with yachts in the summer. Eilean Righ, the largest island, has plenty of pleasant stopping places. Crossing the loch is perhaps safest between Bagh Dun Mhuilig and the southern end of Eilean Righ.

River Add and Loch Crinan 065

Distances Round trip of either 6 or 8km on Loch Crinan; River Add is 5.5km.

LENGTH **13.5km**
OS   **55**
GRADE   **1**

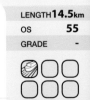

Introduction The small Loch Crinan is the entrance to the Crinan Canal. Crinan Harbour is between an island and the mainland, and the River Add flows into it. One of the main reasons for visiting this area would be Kilmartin Glen, of which the River Add and the surrounding area are important parts, as this was a major gateway into Scotland from Ireland in both pre-Christian and medieval times.

Access From the B841 alongside the Crinan Canal, to Islandadd bridge (804925), or the Crinan Canal basin (789944).

Campsites & accommodation Camping near to the Bellanoch Hotel, just after Islandadd bridge.

Description The Add is quite possible from the road to Dunadd, the obvious hill fort which rises over the very flat plain of Moine Mhor, and it flows a very winding 5.5km into the estuary at Islandadd bridge. 1.5km of sandy / muddy estuary follows until Crinan Ferry, a very obvious ferry point, now disused but of historic interest.
The area of Moine Mhor is the southern part of Kilmartin Glen, with enough cairns, stone circles and cup and ring rocks to keep anybody happy. It is really worthwhile to start at the museum and take a guided tour of the area.

Crinan Canal 066

Portages Portages around four sets of locks (15 locks in all).

LENGTH **14.5km**
OS   **55**
GRADE   **-**

Introduction This canal is 'Scotland's most beautiful shortcut', the 14.5km-long waterway cutting off the 160km trip around the Mull of Kintyre. There are 15 locks, in four groups, leading to four portages, and 7 bridges.

Access The B841 runs alongside the canal to Crinan, the westerly entrance. Egress at Ardrishaig (852852) on the A83 road down the east coast of Kintyre.

Campsites & accommodation At Tayvallich and Lochgilphead, plus at Bellanoch on the canal.

Description The canal runs west to east from Crinan village, past Lochgilphead, to the sea at Ardrishaig. The useful campsite in the centre of Lochgilphead can be reached by a short portage.
Go to the very informative website www.scottishcanals.com for full details.

067 Tayvallich and Loch Sween

LENGTH **34km**
OS   **62/55**
GRADE   -

Distances Round trip of 34km.

Introduction This area has much for paddlers – a very sheltered top end of Loch Sween with inlets to explore, the village of Tayvallich, a yachting centre and harbour, and the Sound of Jura under a kilometre to the west at Carsaig.

Access The B8025 runs from the Crinan Canal to Tayvallich (740872), and a side road leaves this to follow the east side of Loch Sween down to Castle Sween (715790).

Campsites & accommodation At Tayvallich and Castle Sween.

Description The loch is 17km from its head out to the McCormaig Islands, which can be reached in calm weather.
The head has three inlets to paddle. Caol Scotnish gives the experience of both sea and woodland habitat, a heronry in the forest, and woodland birds on rocks in the tidal area. It is not surprising that this wet and wooded habitat has been chosen for the first re-introduction in Scotland of the European beaver (due in 2005/06). Around the corner, on the main loch are the Fairy Islands on the west side, an area of lagoons, sandbars and wooded islands, all peaceful and worth exploring.
About two-thirds of the way down Loch Sween is Castle Sween, a caravan and campsite, with shop. Speedboats may be encountered around here.
On the opposite, west side are two large inlets, both quite hidden. Linne Mhuirich is behind Taynich Island and the Ulva Islands.
A canoe can of course push its nose through narrow passages

and shallow water. Further south is the Island of Danna, hardly recognised, but able to be circumnavigated in calm conditions. Eilean Mor, the largest of the four McCormaigs, is well worth a visit. At one point in history, this was a 'motorway' stop for the sea traffic between Ireland and Scotland, and so it is not surprising that a saint made his home here – the cave, chapel and cross can all be seen.

West Loch Tarbert 068

LENGTH	28km
OS	62
GRADE	-

Distances Round trip of 28km.

Introduction This is the most southerly paddling recommended in this area, and this loch has two things going for it: it has a genuinely short and possible portage from the town of Tarbert over the neck of land to the west, and a very convenient campsite just where you might want to embark.

Access From the A83, which follows the loch down its east side. Access on at the top (843664) near to the campsite. Egress on to a small road off the B8024 on the west side at a bay near the mouth with the sea (755595).

Campsites & accommodation Near the head of the loch (Tarbert).

Description There have been open canoe trips down Loch Fyne, overland west at Tarbert, and up to Loch Killisport or Loch Sween, but, as always, very settled weather is required. The portage is 1.5km, and the loch is 14km long. The paddle is fairly sheltered out as far as Ardpatrick Point, and one good tour is to round the point to Loch Stornoway (3km).

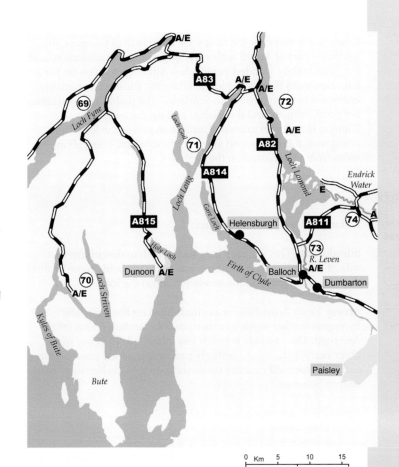

Cowal

069 Loch Fyne 102
070 Isle of Bute and Nearby Lochs 103
071 Lochs Long, Goil, Holy Loch
      and Gare Loch 104
072 Loch Lomond 109
073 Loch Lomond, River Leven, Firth
      of Clyde and Loch Long . . . 111
074 Endrick Water 112

Cowal

Cowal is the name for the land west and north of Glasgow, the southerly part of Argyll with very long road communication, and long and mainly wooded peninsulas. Although a favourite for a long time with the population of Glasgow, the area is relatively unknown to many visitors to Scotland – the paddling possibilities are good, both around the islands and up the long lochs. Dunoon is the main town on Cowal but, unless the ferry from Glasgow is taken, the road journey is enormous, being about 70 miles from Dumbarton on the Firth of Clyde.

069   Loch Fyne

LENGTH   - km
OS **62/55/56**

GRADE   -

Distances The loch is 65km long.

Introduction This is a very long loch which makes up the east side of the peninsula of Kintyre. Interest is probably more in short day trips out from various access points on the loch.

Access From Ardrishaig or Lochgilphead on the west side, Inveraray further north, or other possible landing points off the A83 road. The east side is much less inhabited, with few roads. Otter Ferry is the most southerly practicable access point on the east, a minor road running up its shore to join the Rothesay road near to Strachur.

Campsites & accommodation At Lochgilphead, and two sites just south of Inveraray.

Description Interest for paddlers probably starts at Tarbert, with Ardrishaig (Crinan Canal) 17km to the north. Around the headland protecting Lochgilphead, Loch Fyne heads north-east, Otter Ferry on the east shore (Cowal), being another 8km. The loch narrows to some 1.5-2km wide, and the A83 mainly follows the west shore. It is a long 30km up to Inveraray, the most important town on this stretch of coast, and a further 10km to the head of the loch. From near here, the main road crosses Cowal by the 'Rest and be Thankful' pass to Arrochar, and Tarbet on Loch Lomond. From Strachur, on the east side, it is a 7km portage (possibly using also the River Cur) over to the narrow, 10km long Loch Eck, which has been used in the past to reach Holy Loch, down the River Eachaig. This is a beautiful area with good campsites, and it is quiet and isolated.

Isle of Bute and Nearby Lochs 070

Distances Loch Ruel is 5km long, Loch Striven 13km long. A round trip down one loch, along the Kyles of Bute, and up the other loch is 25km.

LENGTH	**25km**
OS	**63**
GRADE	-

Introduction This is the outermost part of the Firth of Clyde which is suitable for ordinary canoes and kayaks. Bute may be circumnavigated, but the west coast can be rocky, with no roads. The east side is more sheltered, with more habitation, but also more disturbance. The island is more than 50km in circumference. The islands of Great Cumbrae and Little Cumbrae are off to the east, the latter being rocky and exposed. This area is described in one section, because a trip or holiday may be taken in the general area.

Access From Rothesay on Bute, reached by ferry from Wemyss Bay, or by A866 road from Strachur, which follows the Kyle down to its end at Strone Point (075714).

Campsites & accommodation No known formal sites in the immediate area.

Description Loch Ruel is to the north of Bute, only 0.5km away, being 5km long, half of which dries out at low tide. The Kyle is interesting, with islands and shallows. Scenery good in the whole area, very wooded.
Loch Striven is 13km long, a narrow loch which is quite isolated, there being no road up the west side.

071 Lochs Long, Goil, Holy Loch and Gare Loch

LENGTH **42km**
OS   **56/63**
GRADE   -

Distances A trip of 42km on Loch Long and Loch Goil.

Introduction These lochs represent the more interesting and useful paddling in the area of the upper Firth of Clyde. *Take note! All can be affected by naval operations, usually submarine exercises.* The normally restricted area is on the east side of Loch Long, covering the Coulport area. All that paddlers have to do is to avoid this area by crossing over to the west bank well in time. If following the east bank, head across at Peaton Layo (Grid reference NS 214860) to Ardentinny, and keep to the west bank until Loch Goil.

Access The head of Loch Long is reached on the A83, or A814 from Tarbet on Loch Lomond. The B828 and B839 end up at Lochgoilhead, a good base for a trip in these parts.

Campsites & accommodation Lochgoilhead, and Gairletter Point, south of Ardentinny on Loch Long. Ardgarten, at the top of Loch Long.

Description Holy Loch is the most westerly of this foursome, just around the corner from Dunoon, 3.5km long, and heavily populated. It does lead, however, by a portage, to Loch Eck inland. Loch Long is as it sounds, very long, 26km from its entrance opposite Gourock on the Clyde up to Arrochar, from whence a portage may be made over to Loch Lomond. The round trip, in settled weather, from Lomond down the River Leven to the Clyde, along to Loch Long, and over the Arrochar neck back to Loch Lomond, is a long-established touring route. It is a 3-day trip. The first part of Loch Long has roads both sides, but these finish at Ardentinny on the west side, and Coulport on the east, after the first 6km. After another 5km Loch Goil opens out up to the north-west, a gem of an area for touring. This is a very attractive and wooded 8km loch, well worth exploring. The head of the loch at Lochgoilhead is a good base, with a large campsite. Loch Long then stretches for a further 14km to the head, where the main A83 winds around it.
Gare Loch is very busy, and almost industrialised for its 10km length, with the town of Helensburgh, the marina at Rhu, and then the major naval base at Faslane. It is probably best avoided with so many other pleasant cruising grounds nearby.

River Lochy, Ben Nevis in background - www.RayGoodwin.com

Misty morning - www.RayGoodwin.com

Loch Quoich - www.RayGoodwin.com

Loch Laggan - www.RayGoodwin.com

Upper River Garry - www.RayGoodwin.com

Bivvi on the Upper River Garry - www.RayGoodwin.com

Loch Lomond 072

Distances A round trip of at least 72km is posssible.

LENGTH **72km**	
OS	**56**
GRADE	-

Introduction *See Route 071 concerning MoD. restricted areas.* This famous and beautiful loch is a great favourite with canoeists and kayakers, and offers one of the best and most interesting stretches of fresh water in Britain. The loch is large, with both large and small islands and so the paddling possibilities are endless. A week's holiday can easily be spent on it, and the West Highland Way also follows the east bank.
Since 2003 Loch Lomond has been part of the Loch Lomond and Trossachs National Park, although the main change noticed by local paddlers has been an increase in speedboats and jet skis which are a menace, although mainly on weekends in high summer.

Access The loch is also quite different in character, the northerly 'narrow end' being much quieter than the 'bulge' at the southern end, and the fleshpots of Balloch. A main road (A82) follows the west bank, whilst on the east side a road only goes as far as Rowardennan, leading to Ben Lomond, and the famous Youth Hostel there. This means that the east side has quite a few attractions.

Campsites & accommodation
Camping can be difficult, but main sites are mentioned. The islands are private, and camping is usually not allowed.

Description The loch is 36km long, 6kms wide in some places, and over 550m deep. With winds being mainly from the south-west, the fetch can be large, and waves high at times. The weather is also very unpredictable, the loch being surrounded by mountains, and very fast-changing weather. A day trip out to islands should be made with this knowledge in mind. The 30 islands have castles, monuments, and many points of interest. This is a real tourist treat, and so the paddler should take time and explore. Some distances are set out below with some hints for visits.

Km

0   Ardlui - the top of the loch, with access now difficult onto the loch. Launch to the River Falloch about 2km up from the village, much easier.
Going south. The A82 road follows the west bank.

3   I Vow Island. Castle.

5.5   Rob Roy's Cave on left bank.

6.5   Inveruglas Isle to right, Castle.

7.5   Inversnaid on left (east) bank. Gateway to the Trossach lochs. Pier and hotel.

12.5   Tarbet on right bank. 3km portage west to Loch Long. Hotels, shops, pier.

18.5   Rowardennan Lodge (Youth Hostel) on left bank.

19.5   Rowardennan Hotel and car park, picnic site on left bank.

Inverbeg on right bank. Caravan site and pier.

25.5   Ross Point on left. Loch narrows for a final time. Ross Islands to left.

28   On right bank (west) Luss village, shops, pier, sandy beach. To south, Inchlonaig Island.
To south-east (east bank) – Cashel campsite (Forest Enterprise). Beach, landing, room for boats and canoes.

30   On west side, south from Luss, Aldochlay village.
South from Inchlonaig, six islands in the centre of the loch; west to east: Inchtavannach, the 'Lagoon', interesting narrow passage between it and Inchconnachan (the wallaby island – wallabies were released here some years ago); Inchmoan, with good sandy beaches, and Inchgalbraith, a crannog to the south of it; a very narrow and shallow passage between it and Inchcruin, and then Bucinch off to the north; to the east again, Inchfad, with Ellendarroch off its west end, another crannog.

30.5   On east side, Strathcashel Point, then Milarrochy Bay (campsite), with boathouse for Loch Lomond Sailing Club, which houses many sailing canoes.

31   On west side Bandry Bay, look out for the statue in the water.

31.5   South from Inchfad:

Five islands in a line from NE to SW, Inchcailloch, a nature reserve, with a campsite, viewpoint on its hill, chapel at east end; land at sandy bay near to west end. This island well worth visiting.

33   On east side Balmaha village, with marina, shops, cafes, hotels.

There follows Clairinsh, behind and to the south of Inchcailloch, Torrinch to the south-west and Creinch, again to south-west.

It is unlikely that the paddler will really want to go south of these islands, as near to Balloch, the speedboat traffic increases greatly. Inchmurrin is to the south, with a pier, castle, and hotel, the largest island.

To the west are a number of private properties with little landing or egress. There is a jetty due west of the Inchmurrin jetty, and another 2km further south at Arden House.

Cameron House Hotel is 1.5km nearer to Balloch, followed by the new Loch Lomond Shores shopping centre.

Balloch, as hinted at above, can be very busy with many boat movements. It has shopping, and a country park on the east bank. The River Leven leaves the loch through a very congested boat area, and then a weir prevents the motorised boats going any further south. The river winds for 9km through an urban area to the Clyde (risk of children throwing stones), with the latter third tidal. It is only recommended for transit to the Clyde.

Loch Lomond, River Leven, Firth of Clyde and Loch Long   073

LENGTH	**81**km
OS	**56/63**
GRADE	**1**

Portages A portage on the River Leven, down the barrier/weir below Balloch; a portage of 2.5km from Arrochar to Tarbet, between Loch Long and Loch Lomond.

Introduction An absolutely classic trip, carried out many times by the Open Canoe Sailing Group. It involves every type of paddling and sailing.

Access Usually started on Loch Lomond, either at Tarbet or Balloch.

Campsites & accommodation Various places described in the text will enable you to have a quiet night and avoid habitation.

Description This route has been mainly covered in the other trips in the Cowal section. There are few difficulties apart from the exposure of the Firth of Clyde, and the fact that the River Leven is not amongst the most pleasant.

The distances are:

Tarbet to Balloch - 22km.

Balloch to Dumbarton - 12km.

Dumbarton to Ardmore, (possible campsite) after Cardross -10km.

Ardmore, across mouth of Gare Loch to Rosneath Point (stopping place or campsite) - 5km - on to Loch Long - 5km.

Loch Long to Arrochar - 25km (many camping possibilities on Loch Long).

Arrochar, portage across to Tarbet - 2.5km.

Other important points Time taken will be three (hard) days minimum.

074 Endrick Water

LENGTH	**8km**
OS	**56/57**
GRADE	**1**

Introduction The Endrick is small, and probably only of local interest, but many visitors to Loch Lomond have attempted it. It was formerly very prone to the 'angry farmer syndrome' which should have abated. It rises miles to the east in the Stirlingshire hills above Fintry.

Access Near to the east side of Loch Lomond, reached by the road through Drymen. The A809 runs down to Glasgow, and the B834 is off to the east of here. The river can be seen from the road most of the way.

Campsites & accommodation Balmaha on Loch Lomond.

Description It is a pleasant and winding little river amongst very pastoral countryside reminding one of a southern English river. A trip is eminently possible from the road bridge near to Drymen, the 7km down to Loch Lomond, where a 1km paddle would bring you northwards to the harbour at Balmaha. Above Drymen, the highest possible start point is probably west of Killearn, where the Blane Water joins just after the B834 road bridge, an easier access than many, adding another 4km to the distance.

East

East

Moray and Grampian

075 River Nairn 119
076 Upper Findhorn 120
077 Lower Findhorn 122
078 Loch Ericht 123
079 River Spey 123
080 River Deveron 128
081 River Don 130
082 River Dee 132

Tayside

083 Loch Rannoch 139
084 Loch Tummel 140
085 Lower River Tummel 140
086 Loch Daimh 145
087 Loch Lyon 146
088 Upper River Lyon 146
089 Lower River Lyon 147
090 Cononish, Fillan and Dochart 148
091 Loch Tay 150
092 River Tay 151
093 Firth of Tay 155
094 Upper River Isla 156
095 Lower River Isla 158
096 Upper Shee Water 160
097 Lower Ericht 161
098 River Earn 161

Angus

099 Lower North Esk 166
100 Upper South Esk 168
101 Lower South Esk 169
102 Dean Water 171
103 Lunan Water 172

Fife

104 River Eden 176
105 Loch Leven 181
106 River Leven 181

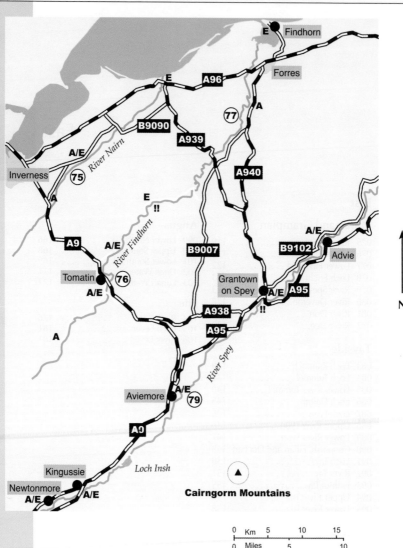

Cairngorm Mountains

N

Moray and Grampian

075 River Nairn. 119
076 Upper Findhorn 120
077 Lower Findhorn 122
078 Loch Ericht. 123
079 River Spey 123

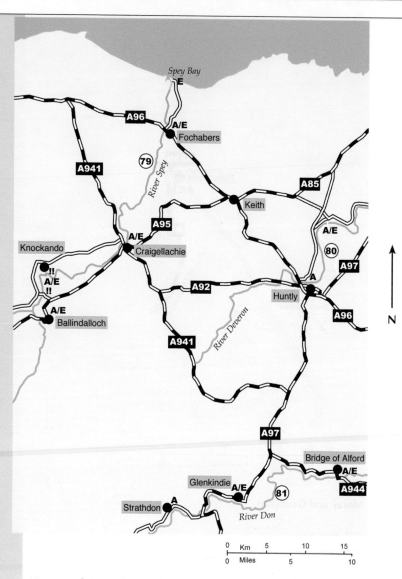

Moray and Grampian continued

079 River Spey 123   081 River Don. 130
080 River Deveron 128

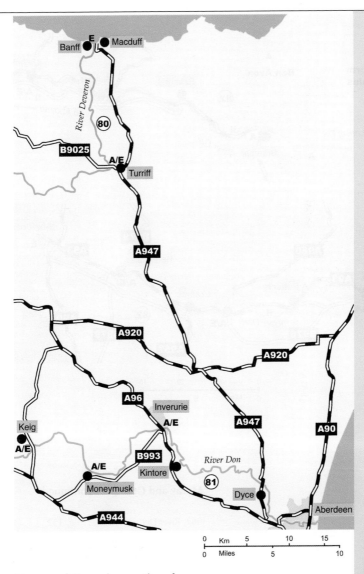

Moray and Grampian continued

080 River Deveron 128
081 River Don. 130

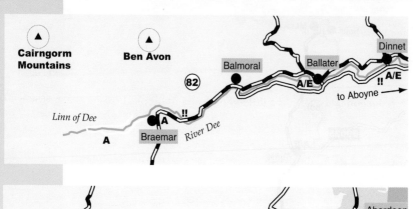

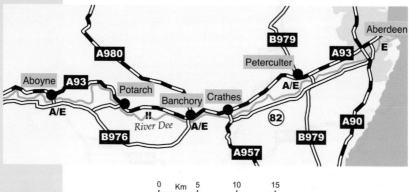

Moray and Grampian continued

082 River Dee 132

Moray and Grampian

River Nairn 075

Introduction The Nairn is a little-known and underused river, flowing down a delightful valley. It rises on the western side of the Monadhliath, above the 'Scottish Lake District' around the eastern side of Loch Ness, and flows north-east to the sea at Nairn town. It is a useful day trip either when other rivers are too high, or the sea is too rough.

LENGTH	**27**km
OS	**27**
GRADE	**1-2**

Water Level Look at any bridge, but especially the B9090 – the river can be paddled if there is enough water over the shingle rapids.

Access The Nairn passes under the main A9 road, and access and parking is at the old road bridge east of the current road (721388). Also access/egress at next road bridge (742430), Clava Lodge Hotel bridge (759448), Cantray bridge (800480), the B9090 road bridge near to Cawdor, and Howford bridge (876538). Final egress in Nairn, last bridge carries the A96 over (886566), or in the harbour (dry at low tide).

Campsites & accommodation Newlands, near to Culloden, at Nairn beach, east of the town, or at Househill, just south of Nairn.

Description The Nairn proceeds north-east 27km to the sea at Nairn town, a long trip for one day, and is an easy grade 1-2, requiring water to make it worthwhile. Little wooded gorges are interspersed with wider, braided stretches with gravel islands. Access/egress only at five road bridges down the valley. The fourth one, (the B9090), is possibly a better start point for an open canoe, due to numerous trees across the river in the upper stretches. The river passes very close to the Culloden Moor battleground, well worthwhile visiting for its atmosphere.

076 Upper Findhorn

LENGTH **27**km
OS   **27/35**
GRADE   **1-2**

Grade Grade 1-2 (but some of the river is very isolated, increasing the seriousness of the grade).

Introduction Yes, this is *'The'* Findhorn, which has an upper valley of some length, and a canoeing possibility of a long day trip above the difficult upper and lower gorges. This upper valley has been ignored in favour of the superb white water stretches lower down, but egress is possible before Dulsie Rapid, the usual start of the white water 'Upper Findhorn'. Perhaps one reason is that no road follows 12km of the river.

Just to make this even more interesting, the conventional upper and middle reaches have been done by open canoe, with just a couple of portages, plus the bottom end below the Lower Gorge from Mains of Sluie down to the sea at Findhorn. If interested, see the Scottish White Water guide, but this is an advanced trip!

Water Level The river is shallow and shingly. A look over the bridge at Findhorn Bridge should save unnecessary driving, the level will be obvious.

Access From the A9 at Tomatin, south of Inverness, for the upper valley, viewing the river at Findhorn Bridge (803277). Egress for this stretch is near Banchor (908403), upstream of Dulsie Bridge, the usual start for white water trips.

Campsites & accommodation None nearby. Carrbridge or Aviemore would be the best bets.

Description
Km

0   At Tomatin, on the A9, turn off for Drumbain and Morile on a side road, just after the Slochd summit coming north. At Findhorn road bridge, cross the river, look at the level, which should be obvious, and head up the valley. The river is wide, flat and shallow. The valley is flat-bottomed, and very remote, there often being no signs of life in this stalking and shooting area. If there is water at all, the river will be doable from Garbole, where a tributary enters. There is a large lay-by here for parking.

2.5   Large islands.

7.5   Findhorn Bridge – nice parking on the bridge where strange concrete abutments have been built. There is now a choice, of going on to the near take-out, some 7.5km downstream at Ruthven, easily reached by road, or on to Carnoch, 12km, and a vehicle shuttle of at least 26 miles!

8.5   Railway bridge, followed by A9 bridge, both very high above valley.
River bends considerably, always near to the A9.

14   Tributary enters left. Just after this, road comes alongside on the left, and there is also a parking space on the left bank. (The rest of road only has passing places – this road comes down from the A9 at Dalmagarry).

15   Ruthven hamlet on left. Road finishes, and hills close in. River remains of same character, rapids maybe grade 2-3 in high water.

17.5 'Sheep trolley' crosses river on ropeway. Shennachie ruin on left.

18   Long bend to right. River narrows and speeds up.

22.5 Approaching sharp bend to left, Daless Farm is high on hill to the left, first road, and egress in emergency.

24   Bridge. Drynachan Lodge on left bank. Road now follows left bank.

25   Carnoch to left.

27   Road is right alongside river - this is easiest place to egress from this trip, and is 2km upriver from Banchor.
The Findhorn now starts to speed up and become more difficult. In another 2.5km is Dulsie Rapid… go and have a look at it from Dulsie bridge.

077 Lower Findhorn (Below Sluie Gorge)

LEN.   **15.5**km
OS   **27**
GRADE   **1-2**

Introduction A beautiful trip, amongst the same staggering scenery as the rest of the Lower Findhorn, ending at Findhorn village, across the estuary.

Water Level Look upstream at A96 road bridge – the steepish rapid upstream should have enough water not to be a scrape.

Access From the A940, Grantown to Forres road, where the car park for the Mains of Sluie walks are signposted (013523), at the main A96 road bridge (011581), and at Findhorn harbour (038645).

Campsites & accommodation Mundole, on the river, and at Findhorn (two sites).

Description

Km

0   Launch at Mains of Sluie, where the lower gorge ends. Vehicles can be taken down to the old farmhouse (now renovated as holiday accommodation, please show regard for others here), and removed to the car park near the main road. This paddle is a glorious one in an easy, wooded, red sandstone gorge.

4   Where the river finally straightens out, after sharp bends and cliffs, is the Meads of St. John on left bank – beautiful ancient trees.

7   Mundole caravan park on right bank, possible egress.

8   Findhorn bridge on A96 – parking and egress on the right upstream of bridge.
     There is now a choice of entering the Findhorn estuary, which runs fast, and leaves large sandbanks at low tide. Only attempt this in high water, and on the last of the flood tide.

9   Railway bridge.

13   River enters estuary proper.
     Head across north to Findhorn village (obvious).

15.5 Findhorn harbour. Campsites at both village and at Findhorn Foundation, a mile inland.

Distances 26km (round trip of 54km).

LENGTH	**26km**
OS	**42**
GRADE	-

Introduction Loch Ericht is included here because, at least geographically, it makes sense to include it with the Spey, the loch being almost the most central loch in Scotland. It actually drains out both north to the Truim, a Spey tributary, and south into the River Ericht, a Tummel and Tay system tributary.

Access From the north, from Dalwhinnie on the A9.
There is also an estate road to the south end (from Bridge of Ericht on Loch Rannoch), which is barred by a locked gate in a deer fence, and although access is allowed at some times, much frustration is caused by paddlers arriving and finding it locked. There is no logical system in place at time of writing.

Campsites & accommodation Wild camping on the loch. The nearest sites are at Dalwhinnie or Newtonmore.

Description The loch is a summer favourite for open canoeists wanting some peace and quiet, and offers 26km of an often wind-swept vista. It is used for mountain access to Ben Alder, which dominates the west side. The Rannoch Forest mountains are to the south-west, and the Drumochter hills to the east.
Access by road is easy via Dalwhinnie to the dam at the north end. The Ben Alder estate allows access, but this is more convenient as it is before its gatehouse. Campsites are easy to find, the infrequent little bays offering shelter.
Down near the southern end, on the west side is Alder Bay, with Ben Alder Cottage, a bothy, and Bonnie Prince Charlie's cave above it.

Grades Grade 1, apart from grade 2 rapids at Grantown, Blacksboat, and Knockando to Carron Bridge.

LEN.	**114km**
OS	**35/36/28**
GRADE	**1(2)**

Introduction Yes, one of the 'Big Four' rivers that is a must for the touring canoeist in Scotland, and which normally provides a fast current, great scenery, and some interesting rapids.
The Spey is also a strange river in that much of the flow in the upper reaches is taken off by the Laggan dam scheme, taking

water west from the watershed. The Spey is rarely done from up by Laggan village, more normally from either Newtonmore or Kingussie. Many prefer to start from Clive Freshwater's Loch Insh Centre, but this would miss out the Insh marshes, which are worth seeing.

The Spey can easily be paddled in two and a half days in medium water from Newtonmore, but on high winter days, the river from the Avon junction down to the sea can be paddled (all 40km of it!) easily in a day by either kayak or canoe.

In recent years, middle summer levels have meant a deal of wading for parties of open canoeists, many feeling that the river is losing water, probably due to abstraction, but it is still a great experience, with the definite feeling that the river speeds up near the sea.

The river is described from Newtonmore, with campsites in the itinerary. Day trips on parts of the river are also well worthwhile.

Possible Itineraries

1) Newtonmore (campsite) to Aviemore (campsite) - 29km.
Aviemore to Blackboats (campsite, booked in advance) - 35km.
Blackboats to Spey Bay (campsite) - 40km.

2) Loch Insh (accom.) to Boat of Balliefurth - 31.5km.
Balliefurth to Blackboats - 24.5km or Boat of Fiddich, Craigellachie campsite - 35.5km.
To Spey Bay, either 40, or 29km.

Water Level Look at level at Newtonmore and Kingussie. There should be enough depth over the gravel rapids.

Access Details of the access points are in the text. Please keep to these, and take heed of advice. The Spey is a fine river for both canoeists and anglers, and can be crowded in places.

Description

Km

0   Spey Bridge campsite, (709980) Newtonmore (just off the A9). Village is 0.5km north. If river is obviously very dry, consider the next 8km carefully. Rapid just below campsite. Railway bridge. The river is small, with gravel banks and islands. Access either left bank below bridge if using campsite or right bank.

8   Kingussie bridge (760997). By now, you're exhausted, and thinking this will take a week! River enlarges. Access right bank, below Ruthven road bridge.

9   A9 bridge. River enters Insh marshes, and scenery widens out. If low, view is obscured by high banks; if high, river is out over the marshes. Much bird life.

17   River enters Loch Insh. The watersports centre is obvious on right bank (838045). Landing, bar, restaurant, lodges for rent.

19   Kincraig bridge at end of loch (835056). River speeds up. Access right bank below bridge (park in large lay-by opposite church), and access 100m downstream over rough track running parallel with road.

20   Gravel islands where River Feshie enters from right.

29   Aviemore bridge (894116). Access left bank below road bridge. There is a campsite at Coylumbridge, 2km to the right – possible, but a haul if tired! This first stretch of 29km can be paddled in 5 to 8 hours, making a good first day or half day. From here to Grantown is slow and deep.

40   Boat of Garten bridge (946191). Access left bank downstream of road bridge. Island below, good for a stop.

46   After a long, straight stretch, often subject to winds, is Broomhill Bridge (998224) - Nethy Bridge village to right. Access left bank. There is a campsite soon, if tired!

47.5   River Dulnain joins from left.

48   Some standing stones appear on left bank, telling you that Boat of Balliefurth campsite is near.

48.5   Boat of Balliefurth on right bank (013245). A sign tells you that canoeists are welcome. Camping is on the bank, with a farmyard at the back, with cold water tap, and toilet. Proprieters will come down and take money, and have been very helpful and friendly - their house is some 500m away. This campsite can be a useful distance for a first night's camp if starting from Loch Insh (30km).

52   Grantown road bridge -A939 (034268). Good landing and parking just before bridge on left. Rocks appear in river, warning of the long and interesting Grantown rapid ahead after bridge. It is an easy to inspect grade 2, finishing below the old bridge 0.5km below.

56.5 After a pleasant wooded stretch in a deep valley, Cromdale
      bridge (066289), village to right. Access right bank below
      road bridge, by the church. The next 10 or 11km are fast-
      flowing, with good scenery.

58.5 Island.

60   Road near on right bank.

61   Dellefure Burn on left, and road. Limited access and parking
      (085316) .

64   Islands.

66   Advie bridge (120354), landing and parking on left bank,
      park on verge opposite 5-bar gate. Pretty wooded stretch
      with islands follows, shallow in low water. Possible rough
      campsites in woods after another 2km.

71   Road alongside on left bank, Dalnapot (known as Ballindal-
      loch 1). Good parking spots (158370) for starting a trip on
      the faster stretches coming up. Please try and avoid this very
      popular spot if possible, and move vehicles quickly. From
      this spot, a day trip of some 17km down to Aberlour will
      give any canoeist or kayaker a very good day trip. This is
      reached by coming off the A95, over Blacksboat bridge on
      the B9138, and turning left up the valley for some 3km. The
      other Ballindalloch parking place is for those using the Spey-
      side Way campsite, by the old station, right bank – access on
      left bank just below old railway bridge (169369), as below.

71.5 Old railway bridge, Long Distance Footpath goes over.

72   River Avon (pronounced 'Ayon') joins from right, heralded
      by far faster water than so far encountered.

73   The first gripping experience for those in open canoes, the
      rapid known as Blacksboat Rapid, the 'Washing Machine', or
      various other names. A good grade 2 ramp between shingle
      banks, with a long wave train. Even in medium flows, this
      rapid can fill a canoe.

74   Blacksboat bridge (184390). Camping is allowed at the old sta-
      tion on the left (take out above bridge on left), but there are no
      facilities. Ballindalloch Estate have to be contacted first.

76.5 Fast water down to Knockando (19041416). When bends, a
      first island, and the old distillery chimney come into sight,
      you are nearly there. The rapids are not difficult, the middle

channel normally taken, ending in a drop near to the left
bank. There is landing immediately below, and steps up to
the car park. This is an SCA facility, but it is envisaged that
touring paddlers will only pass through.
In the next 4km are 5 further rapids, all interesting and
obvious, large waves in high water, down to Carron. Scenic
wooded valley.

80.5 Carron bridge (225411). Access left bank by bridge.

83.5 The last of the series of rapids with an appreciable drop.

85   Charlestown of Aberlour village to right, footbridge
      (262429), park on right bank, with vehicle access. Shallow
      stretch to next bridge.

88.5 Craigellachie old bridge, followed by new road bridge, rapid
      under. Access from car park on right bank (286451).
      Just downstream of the rapid, on the right bank, is a landing
      with parking nearby, and Boat O'Fiddich campsite. Leave
      vehicles across road in Fiddich Park, where there are toilets.
      Another formal campsite is 2.5km away, at the back of Aber-
      lour village. Whilst a very pleasant site, it really requires a
      vehicle, or a very long and uphill trolley portage.
      This last 24km to the sea can be completed in a half day. For
      many kilometres, the bulk of Ben Aigan on the right bank
      dominates the scenery.

91   The A941 on left bank, parking.

93.5 Rothes to the left, no easy access.
      After shallow gravel rapids, two sudden drops just before
      Boat O'Brig.

99   Boat O'Brig road and rail bridges. Access left bank, above or
      below road bridge (318516).
      The river now unexpectedly enters a scenic stretch with
      islands, and good stopping places, and the dramatic red
      sandstone cliffs of the 'Seven Pillars of Hercules' on the right
      bank. There can be sudden winds whilst under the cliffs.

104   HT power lines cross the river, viewpoint on the cliffs far
      above. Only 3km to Fochabers.

107   Fochabers village to right, park with access and parking on
      right bank.

107.5 Fochabers bridge, A96 trunk road. Access on right, below
      bridge (341596), via a track from the riverside road. The

scenery changes again, to a flat, gravelly bed, with many islands. Still a fast current.

111   Easy to get lost amongst little gravel runs and islands with shrubs in the summer.

112.5 Disused railway bridge, now used as footbridge. A sign you are nearly at the end!

113.5 Surprisingly, the tidal limit, with the sea at Spey Bay in sight. One of the most unusual estuaries in the UK.
On the right bank, landing, to reach the car parking, Visitor Centre (349656), museum, and Tugnet Icehouse. Great mounds of shingle. All facilities at centre, including a really good café.

114   The open sea. Shallows, sandbanks and channels to the left. There is a campsite next to the Spey Bay Hotel, 0.5km to right. The hotel has also kept an eye on cars belonging to paddlers whilst completing the river.

080 Deveron

LENGTH **50km**
OS   **29**
GRADE   **2**

Portages Possible portages at Milltown of Rothiemay (400m) and Marnoch Lodge bridge (400m).

Introduction This little-known and charming river gives the paddler some nearly 50km of canoeing through the Banff and Buchan countryside. The countryside is quite isolated, being mixed farming and forest, with few facilities. There are no campsites actually on the river, the nearest being a caravan site at Turriff. A better bet, if wishing to make a camp base in the area, is to go to the coast to the north. The scenery is mixed, with wooded gorges and small farms, and in high water gives a fast and flat paddle. The last part to the sea is still scenic, with a very short estuary.

The Deveron rises on The Buck, the main peak in the Ladder Hills on the Moray/Aberdeenshire border, and flows north and east towards Huntly. It has been kayaked from Haugh of Glass, off the Dufftown road, 14km down to Huntly, where the river is a bouldery grade 2-3. For open canoes, the 9km further to the confluence with the Isla is still boulder-strewn, with many small weirs, and a start near to Milltown of Rothiemay is recommended.

Water Level Look at shallows either near to Huntly at the start, or over the bridge at Turriff, to gauge an idea of depth of water.

Access The area of the highest start point is reached from the A96 main Aberdeen to Inverness road near to Huntly, where the river is first seen (515408). As far as Turriff, roads are rarely near to the river, but the final section is followed by a minor road on the east bank, and then the A97 near to Banff, with the final egress at the road bridge between Banff and Macduff (695638).

Campsites & accommodation Turriff. Otherwise, coastal sites west of Banff.

Description

Km

0   Road on left bank (535476).
       River Isla joins.

1.0   Road close to left bank.
       Inspect next 400m. Small rocky weir, followed by rough water, island, and further broken weir.

1.5   Milltown of Rothiemay bridge.
       Picturesque and unspoilt village to left.
       River bends to right, then a long bend to left, to head north, in deep wooded valley.

9.5   Road on left bank, river heads east.

10.5   Marnoch village on left bank.

12.0   Tight bends to right and then left, 400m of rocky water down to bridge. Marnoch Lodge bridge. Access probably on left side. There are no more rapids from here to the sea.
       Kinnairdy Castle on left bank.
       River heads south, then east.

16.5   Burn joins from right.
       Farm roads on both sides, ford.
       Bend to left, large island, pass right side.

20.5   Minor road on right bank.

28.0   Major road, B9025 on right bank, approaching Turriff.

29.0   Turriff bridge, town on hill to right. Rapid under bridge.
       River slows and meanders, but good current in high water.

There are no more public road bridges between here and Banff.

33.0 Island, take right channel.

37.0 Road on right bank.

44.0 Bridge of Alvah, ancient road bridge – access out on right bank, through private road and farm.

47.0 Woodland walks on left bank, river pretty and wooded, islands. No easy access out to road.

47.5 River becomes tidal.

49.5 Final road bridge, Banff Bay. Banff town to left, MacDuff to right. Egress on left side, upsteam of bridge. Very small lay-by here, but parking is better over main road on Bridge Road. (If river is low and tide is out, this last 2km can be problematic due to shallows).

081 River Don

LENGTH **91**km

OS   **37/38**

GRADE   **1/2**

Introduction The Don is of quite an exceptional length and nearly 100km of this length might be canoeable. Unfortunately it does not carry the same volume of water as its neighbour, the Dee to the south. So, if caught high, the Don gives some delightful paddling through pretty rather than spectacular countryside, but it has to be paddled in times of snow-melt or immediately after heavy rain. In the middle reaches, the river needs to be full, almost to the top of the banks.

Water Level The river should be inspected in the middle or higher stretches. The Don needs a lot of water to be navigable for all its length, often full to the banks, otherwise there can be much wading required.

Access The Don rises in the empty mountain area just to the east of the Cairngorm Avon valley, and flows mainly east to the sea. From Corgaff bridge (264088), the river is twisty and rocky, but has been paddled in high water. This is easier by kayak than canoe. Just before Strathdon village is a narrow gorge with falls. After this first 23km is a car park and toilets at Bellabeg (353131), which is the west side of the straggling Strathdon village. This is a convenient start point in high water for experienced open canoeists. However, the river is still frequently rocky for the 9km down to Glenbuchat Castle, with a weir just upstream of the first road bridge over the A944. No easy access at either this bridge or the one 2km downstream. Distances are given from Glenbuchat, but a more sensible start can be made at Glenkindie.

Other access points given in the text. Final egress at Bridge of Don in Aberdeen (945094).

Campsites & accommodation The only obvious and active campsite in the whole area is Haughton House and Country Park (582170) at Alford, run by Aberdeenshire Council, from which launching is also possible.

Description

Km

0   Glenbuchat Castle left. Water of Buchat joins from left. Valley opens out. Parking on flat ground by river.

2.5   Footbridge.

4.0   Islands, then road bridge, B-road, Glenkindie village on left. Car parking on left.

7.0   Road bridge. Milltown of Towie on left. No easy parking.

11.0   Road bridge, Mill of Brux on right, parking on left.

13.5   Farm bridge.

17.5   Brux foot bridge. Steep wooded slopes for next few kilometres. The A944 is present now on left bank - frequent lay-bys for parking. River can be shallow and rocky.

21.0   Farm bridge and church on left.

26.0   Bridge of Alford. A944. Alford village 2km right. No easy access or egress, busy main road.

28.0   Minor road bridge, Montgarrie village, access possible. Aberdeenshire Council campsite 1km on right in country park. Possible launching from park, 0.5km downstream from this bridge. This is reached by driving right through the caravan park, launching, and leaving vehicles in car park by Haughton House.

34   Oakbank road bridge. River now enters a wooded gorge, many minor rapids. This bridge is high, no easy access.

35   Weir, followed by footbridge.
       A further 2km on, a launch point near to Glenton would give

a nice run through the valley, but parking is difficult.

38.5   Mill of Tillefoure on left bank. Road on left, footbridge. Best possible launch site for this stretch.
Hill on left has many pleasant walks.

41   Donview car park (FC) on left, but no access to river.

42.0   Possible parking on bank, at ornamental gates.
Broken weir, followed by 0.5km of rapids.

44   Road bridge, river now slows down. Monymusk village on right, 2km.
Most paddlers with experience now describe the Don as being slow, meandering and tedious, with some pollution. Distances down to Aberdeen are given below.

50.0   Kemnay, road bridge.

59   Main A96 road bridge (high). Weir just before this. Next 2km, various egresses from river, road on right bank and River Urie joins from left.

64.0   Kintore road bridge.

72.0   Hatton of Fintray road bridge.

79.0   Dyce road bridge (A947). Several weirs follow.

85   Aberdeen (Bucksburn) road bridge.

91   Aberdeen (Bridge of Don) road bridge.

082   River Dee

LEN.   **105**km
OS **43/44/38**
GRADE **1(2-3)**

Grade Grade 1 for most of length; grade 2-3 at Invercauld, Dinnet, and between Potarch and Banchory.

Introduction The Dee is one of the four big rivers in Scotland, providing long canoe-camping trips, although it tends to carry the least water. It is characterised by long, stony, shallow rapids, but in condition provides beautiful scenery, and like much of the north-east, there is a sense of comparative isolation and little population. This applies especially in the spring and autumn when water is likely to be the best, but an advantage of the north-east climate can be very dry winter trips, with the river still up enough. October is especially recommended, as the autumn colours are at their best, and the fishing season nearly over. The

Dee rises on the Lairig Ghru, the major pass in the Cairngorms to the west of Ben Macdui, and reaches the sea at Scotland's third city, Aberdeen.

Water Level For open canoes, the river down to Balmoral can often be quite dry, and a start below here is recommended. The river needs to be obviously up at any of the rapids inspected.

Access The river valley is conveniently followed by the A93 for most of its length.

Campsites & accommodation There are, very conveniently, campsites at Ballater and Banchory, to give a superb 3-day trip, but groups have taken four days, and rough camping is possible in many places. As the valley is open, parking for vehicles near to the river is mainly easy.

Description

Km

0 Victoria Bridge, opposite Mar Lodge (4km downstream from Linn of Dee, the highest possible start-point (this stretch grade 2-3). Road comes near to river upstream of bridge. The river is broad and shallow, with shingle.

6 Braemar on right. A touristy little town, most facilities, and a campsite to the south, away from the river.

11.5 Invercauld Bridge. The next part must be inspected, 400m of grade 2-3, depending on height. Awkward rocky passage in an open canoe.
River now virtually alongside road (A93), so inspection for water is quite easy.

21.5 Crathie bridge.

32.5 River Gairn joins left. Several rapids on this stretch before Ballater.

35 River Muick joins right. Much more water in river after this point.

36 Ballater campsite left, and village.
Ballater road bridge. Egress on right above bridge.
The next section to Dinnet has fast water below Cambus O'May, and rapids before Dinnet.

41   Valley narrows, road and cycle path on left bank. Access.
      Cambus O'May is the name of the next stretch of fast water.

42   Footbridge, old Victorian suspension bridge. Access/egress
      both sides at bridge. Parking on left bank. Hotel over the
      main road.

44   Several rocky rapids, gradually building up.

47   Heavy, rocky rapid and drop before Dinnet bridge, on left-hand
      bend. Egress best before bridge on right bank, up farm track.

48   Dinnet bridge. High drop, access awkward.
      Three sections with islands in next stretch down to Aboyne.
      River quietens down.

55   Aboyne bridge. Town to left, egress left below bridge.

60   Large islands.

63   Main road on left bank.

64   Kincardine O'Neil village to left.

67   Potarch bridge. Large rapid above bridge in high water.
      Parking on left above bridge. Potarch Hotel on right bank.
      Start of very popular run down to Banchory.
      First 2km flat water. Bend to left, small rapids commence.

68   Lay-by on left bank, avoids some of the flat stretch if doing
      just this part.

69   Next 4km regular easy rapids in pretty wooded scenery.
      Many fishing lodges and croys.

73   At bend to left, river obviously drops more, and is rocky.
      Cairnton Rapid has a first drop which looks awkward, but
      drops easily into further waves. Inspect left.
      At the point where the waves finish, a rocky right bank can be
      seen, the indicator of Invercannie Rapid. Inspect on right side.

74   Invercannie Rapid drops near to right bank, with one large
      drop, large wave, and breakouts on right, followed in 100m
      by another rapid down right side. Waterworks obvious
      on left bank. This first drop and wave can swamp an open
      canoe. The difficulty probably rises to grade 3 in high water,
      but open canoes usually shoot this with no bother.
      Several rapids down to Banchory, all artificially built up
      with walls for fishing.

76.5 Banchory bridge. Campsite on left below bridge.
      Easy grade 1 rapids from now on.

82   Durris road bridge, Crathes to left. Egress on left below
      bridge.

87   Keiths Muir bridge.

93.5 Peterculter village left. Egress left by path below church.

95   Road bridge (B979). Valley now feeling more built up.

103   Bridge of Dee. Tidal limit. Aberdeen city limits.

104   Road bridge.

105   Railway bridge.

105.5 Road bridge, followed by Aberdeen Boat Club boathouse on
      right bank.
      Compulsory egress, due to Aberdeen Harbour Regulations.

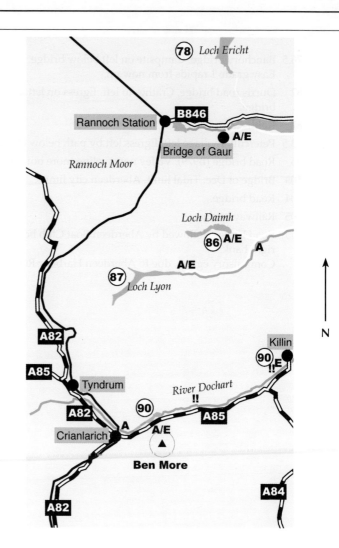

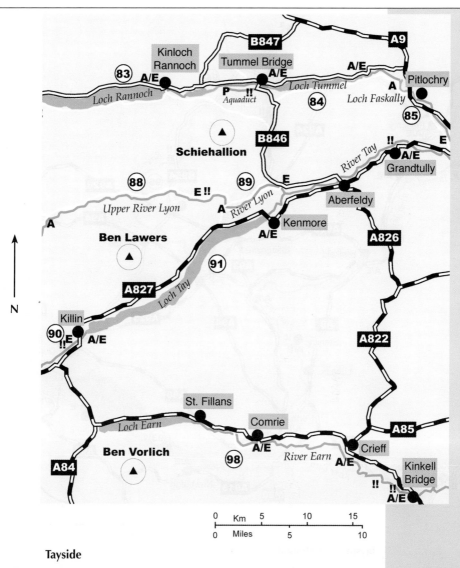

Tayside

083 Loch Rannoch 139
084 Loch Tummel 140
085 Lower River Tummel. 140
086 Loch Daimh 145
087 Loch Lyon. 146
088 Upper River Lyon 146
089 Lower River Lyon 147
090 Cononish, Fillan and Dochart 148
091 Loch Tay. 150
098 River Earn. 161

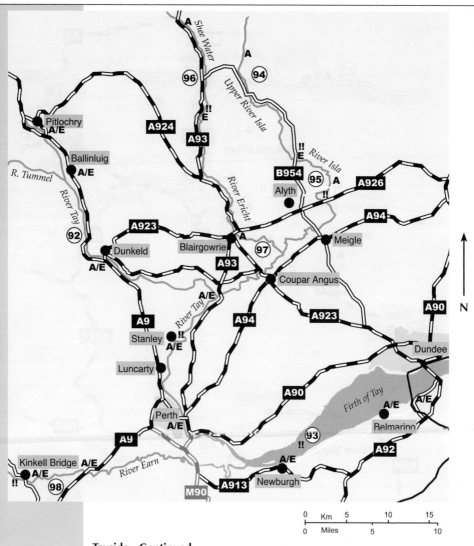

Tayside - Continued

092 River Tay. 151
093 Firth of Tay 155
094 Upper River Isla 156
095 Lower River Isla 158
096 Upper Shee Water 160
097 Lower Ericht. 161
098 River Earn. 161

Tayside

The Tay catchment is one of the largest, if not the largest, in Scotland, and a long touring trip can be planned, using either the Dochart, Loch Tay and River Tay route, or the Rannoch, Tummel and Tay valleys.

Loch Rannoch 083

Distances Round trip of 30km.

LENGTH	**30**km
OS	**42**
GRADE	-

Introduction A loch with a wild feel, but also quite near to civilisation. Part of a major cross-Scotland route.

Access Loch Rannoch can be accessed either at Bridge of Gaur (501567), at its western end, or from the B846 on the north shore (5157), a few kilometres east, or near to Kinloch Rannoch at the eastern end, where the road nears the loch, and has parking (659578).

Campsites & accommodation Tummel Bridge to the east.

Description The loch is 15km long, with relatively few places to egress, but there are plenty of stopping places. It is a favourite second home area for Scots from the central belt, and has almost a Canadian feel with its surrounding wooded mountains.
At the eastern end is a weir within a sluice gate, which can be carried around on the left, or a landing made on the right side some 100m away, followed by the road bridge carrying a minor road over to Aberfeldy to the south. Kinloch Rannoch village to left, with hotels etc, and a community café and post office.
2.5km of river carry the paddler down to Dunalastair Loch, with islands and trees, and then a 1.5km narrow stretch to the dam. In days gone by, canoes were portaged down the road on the left bank to Loch Tummel – definitely not recommended nowadays! The river is a difficult, rocky, and horrible portage in the gorge, but the saving grace is the track following the aqueduct down to the right. This aqueduct has been paddled in the past, but is definitely out of bounds now, and fencing has been erected to discourage this – a fast end to such a trip could be fatal, anyway, in the turbines! The track is 4km long, and leaves the aqueduct halfway down. The end is at Tummel Bridge, and there are 1.5km of shallow river before Loch Tummel.

084 Loch Tummel

LENGTH **22km**	
OS **43/52**	
GRADE **-**	

Distances Round trip of 22km.

Introduction A loch with more of a 'closed-in' feel than Rannoch, as it is narrower, and much more wooded.

Access The B8019 runs along the north side, but physical access is not easy. It is better from Tummel Bridge, south side (7659), the sailing club, south side (798587), or near to the Clunie Dam at the east end (884602).

Campsites & accommodation At Tummel Bridge, Queen's View on the north side, or at Pitlochry to the east.

Description The loch is 11km long, with a sailing club on the south shore, and roads on both banks. Near to the eastern end is Queen's View, a viewpoint and visitor centre, with camp and caravan site. Egress is at the Clunie Dam, on the south shore (some parking). The loch is quite narrow just west of Queen's View, with wooded islands.

085 Lower River Tummel

LENGTH **9.5km**	
OS **52**	
GRADE **1**	

Introduction The River Tummel (SW) between Loch Tummel and Loch Faskally (flooded by the Pitlochry Dam) is kayaked often, and is now rafted, although very narrow in places. It used to be paddled by intrepid soft-skinned kayakers in days gone by, difficult to imagine nowadays, as the final kilometre or so is difficult, and has to be portaged.

Water Level The Tummel is usually very shallow and stony – inspection from the A9 bridge over the river on the Pitlochry bypass will tell you if there looks to be enough water.

Access At the end of the Tummel is Faskally Reservoir, access from the car park at the power station, which looks private, but there is public access through an archway, and down a drive (914597). Egress is at Ballinluig bridge, west side on to minor road, with parking (976521).

Time for a nap - Inspirational Coaching

River Spey - www.standingwaves.co.uk

River Spey - Inspirational Coaching

Loch Affric - Inspirational Coaching

River Spean - Inspirational Coaching

River Spean - Inspirational Coaching

Campsites & accommodation In and around Pitlochry (three large sites).

Description It is 3km down to the dam and fish ladders at Pitlochry from the Faskally Loch car park. Just opposite the launch point, the River Garry joins from the Killiecrankie Pass, which could be launched on to from the Garry bridge 1km upstream. The Loch Faskally start means a long portage at Pitlochry Dam. An easier trip is perhaps from a campsite and minor road bridge below the dam.
The Tummel relies on dam releases, and is often dry in summer - it is a flat and stony grade 1 for 6.5km down to the junction with the Tay below Ballinluig.

Loch Daimh 086

Distances Round trip of 12km.

LENGTH	**12**km
OS	**51**
GRADE	-

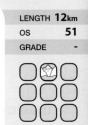

Introduction This isolated loch stands in a wild and bare landscape amongst mountains, at the end of a 3km side road north off the Glen Lyon road.

Access Approached either by the very long road up Glen Lyon from Aberfeldy and Fortingall, or by the fairly new road from the south, via Killin and Glen Lochay, to the unsignposted turn off to the loch (538457), and up to the dam (510464).

Campsites & accommodation There are none in Glen Lyon. The nearest is at either Killin or Aberfeldy.

Description The loch is some 6km long, offering a lonely possibility for wild camping at its head. There are four small islands, if the loch is drawn down. It is a reservoir for Scottish and Southern Energy, and the road has ample parking at its end for both walkers and anglers. From the end of the road, at a locked gate, it is a stiff climb up the height of the dam with a canoe or kayak.

087 Loch Lyon

LENGTH **16**km
OS   **51**
GRADE   **-**

Distances Round trip of 16km.

Introduction Loch Lyon is similar to Loch Daimh in landscape, being at the end of the longest glen road in Scotland, some 35km long. Again, a road takes walkers nearly to the dam, and it is the right-hand side (north) that should be aimed for, as a farm track follows the lochside for most of its length.

Access From the road up Glen Lyon from Aberfeldy and Fortingall, or over the hills from the south from Killin, to the dam (460420).

Campsites & accommodation There are none in Glen Lyon. The nearest is at either Killin or Aberfeldy.

Description The mountains to the west form the boundary between Perthshire and Highland (Glen Orchy). There are two interesting arms of the loch, to the north-west and south-west at the west end, the latter giving a total length for paddling of some 8km. This branch is perhaps the most interesting for landing and camping as the north-west one has more farming activity.

088 Upper River Lyon

LENGTH **18**km
OS   **51**
GRADE   **1-2**

Introduction The River Lyon has possibilities, the upper glen being far more open scenery than the gorge lower down. This is a peaceful upper glen area.

Water Level Obvious at the start – the shingle rapids need to be covered.

Access From the road up the glen, the start being where the Allt Conait joins, near to where the road leaves up to Loch Daimh (529445). Egress is where the road is alongside the river, before the obvious rocky gorge (700472).

Campsites & accommodation None local. The nearest are at Aberfeldy or Killin.

Description From Loch Lyon, going downstream, the first 11km, to the junction with the Allt Conait are rocky, and carry two subsidiary dams, and the small Stronuich reservoir, with slab rapids below it.

Where the burn joins, water increases, and there follows some 18km or so of delightful river to where the white water stretch commences. Some of this is difficult of access due to high wire fences, and egress should always be planned with care at a roadside stretch of river. Reasonable water is required – if the shingle rapids are covered well, the level is good.

Lower River Lyon 089

Introduction The Lower Lyon is a stretch from Bridge of Lyon, the take-out for the white water part, down to the bridge near Keltneyburn, where the Kenmore road leaves the B846, and if desired, on to the Tay.

LENGTH	**6km**
OS	**51**
GRADE	**1(2-3)**

Water Level The rapid downstream of Bridge of Lyon needs to be covered.

Access The start at Bridge of Lyon (729467) has very scarce parking, the egress at Comrie Castle (786488) has a lay-by next to the river, downstream of the bridge.

Campsites & accommodation Aberfeldy.

Description This 6km stretch is both lovely, and an ideal introduction for open canoeists to an interesting grade 2-3 rapid. The rest is grade 1. The trip from Bridge of Lyon down to the Tay, and on to Aberfeldy is an ideal day trip if the water is high enough. The best way to judge this is downstream from Bridge of Lyon. If the shingle is well-covered, the river is high enough.

There are no difficulties, apart from near the end, when pylons are clearly visible, and river narrows. A first minor drop leads round a corner to the right, the second drop has a definite fall on the right side of river, and a couple more small drops follow, between rocks. The pylon line crosses the river halfway down a 400m stretch of rapids. After a flat pool is a second shallow stretch, but no drops. At the end of this, the Keltneyburn joins on the left.

090 Cononish, Fillan and Dochart

LEN.   **21.5**km
OS   **50/51**
GRADE   **2-3**

Portages Two possible portages, at Corriechaorach and Lix rapids.

Introduction This river gives a nice paddling introduction to the Tay, the Dochart being a pretty river with a couple of good rapids (grade 2-3). The valley is many people's introduction to the West Highlands, as they drive up the A82 through Crianlarich and Tyndrum.

Water Level At the Lix rapids, visual inspection should show that they are easily paddled.

Access From the A82, access at Crianlarich (385255), and egress above the Falls of Dochart (563318). A minor road follows the north bank down the lower stretch, useful for inspecting the Lix rapids.

Campsites & accommodation At Tyndrum, Killin, and on Loch Tay.

Description The river initially rises in the corrie of Ben Lui, a spectacular Munroe to the south of Tyndrum, and is known as the Cononish until the bridge at Dalrigh (SW), which was on the old road. This upper river is hardly navigable by kayaks. It then becomes the Fillan, and flows the 5km down the flat valley to Crianlarich, and a further 2km to Loch Dochart. Access and egress on this stretch is only by private roads to houses or campsites. For historical reasons, distances are given from the railway bridge at Crianlarich.

Km

0   Crianlarich railway bridge. Access down a grass track, just downstream of the bridge over the A85, on north side. No camping allowed now, but parking is good on that side of the main road. There is a village store, Post Office, and railway station nearby. (When I was looking at this site again, an elderly man came up to me, and said that he remembered canoeists coming here before WW2, he thought in 1938. They were from England, had of course come by train, and they trolleyed their soft-skinned kayaks and gear down from the railway station, and camped beside the river. The man envied them (he was about 20 then), but he never took up canoeing!).

The river is absolutely flat down to the loch, and is like a canal.

2   River enters Loch Dochart – islands and castle on upper loch, short river to lower loch.

5   Parking and picnic site off A85, a very convenient place to start.

6   The loch gradually starts to move, and become a river again. Wooded and pretty.

7   Private road bridge to Loch Dochart estate and house.

8   Road bridge to Auchessan Farm, much used by walkers and climbers. Minor rocky rapids.

10.5 Rapid at Corriechaorach starts on left, moves over to centre. Quite shootable in open canoe with care.

12   Bridge over to Inishewan. River meanders a bit more, islands.

14.5 Auchlyne road bridge. Some parking, and access on to river. River now very much slows down as far as the Lix rapids. Meanders over a flat plain. B-road on left bank.

20   Woodland starts on right bank, giving warning of the approaching rapids, which start immediately where left bank is wooded, and road is right alongside. Lix Toll junction on A85 is on right bank, 1km.
      Two main drops, followed by a rocky stretch over some 500m. Not difficult with good steering. Bottom of rapids is a good place to take out, unless intending to also do the Falls of Dochart (usually graded 4 plus, and for many years thought to be uncanoeable).

21.5 Lay-by on B-road, last take-out. 1km into Killin village, where there are hotels, tea shops, shops etc.
      (There is another lay-by on right bank, to take out to the A827, Lix Toll to Killin road, but it is very difficult to see!)

091 Loch Tay

LENGTH **48**km

OS **51**

GRADE **48**

Distances Round trip of 48km.

Introduction Loch Tay is some 24km long, running to the north-east from Killin, and then with a bend to the north, and finally to the east, to the end at Kenmore, where the River Tay leaves. Together with the Tay, this is a possible 5-day trip with usually reliable water, and great scenery.

Access Access to the loch is usually from the Killin Hotel car park (573334) on to the short River Lochay (also possible for some 4km down from a road bridge below a fall, but often low in water). Permission should be asked for this, and vehicles removed after access. The A827 follows the north side of the loch, but not very often near to the water. Access/egress also at Fearnan (715443), and at Kenmore, several places near to the watersports centre and car park (7745).

Campsites & accommodation At Killin and Kenmore.

Description The loch is worth a 2-day trip with camping. The scenery is fine, and very different from the road along the north side. A short day's paddle would bring you to the woodland, and waterfall 19km along, opposite Ardreonaig on the south shore (outdoor centre here). Camping possible here. Along most of the loch the roads and human habitation are not very visible. The road comes alongside on the north side near to Fearnan after 18km. (Outdoor centre here also).
Kenmore provides a castle, two crannogs (iron age lake dwell-ings), a watersports centre, car parking, two hotels, and the entrance to the Tay, with a camp and caravan site on the left.

River Tay 092

LENGTH **75**km
OS **51/52/53**
GRADE **1-2(3)**

Grade Grade 1-2, except Grandtully and Stanley, grade 3.

Portages Both Grandtully and Stanley can be avoided, the former by portaging on the right bank just downstream of the house, the latter by portaging using the mill leat.

Introduction The Tay is another Scottish classic, keeping its level much better than other long rivers due to its massive catchment area, the existence of Loch Tay, and its headwaters being virtually on the wet west coast. The river gives 75km of paddling, usually without any portage or wading, and a further 40km of estuary. There are two famous stretches of white water, Grandtully and Stanley, which can be coped with by the bold (see Scottish White Water). The rest are easy grade 2 rapids.
Communication is easy up the Tay valley, with the A9 and A827 near for most of the way, so vehicle shuttles are straightforward.

Water Level The Tay can be paddled in almost any water, and for much of the year tends to be high when other rivers have lost their water. A look at the river at Grandtully from the bank gives a good idea of level, as does the SEPA gauge (SCA website).

Access Kenmore (772456), Aberfeldy (851494), Edradynate – SCA Access Point (888518), Grandtully (911531), Logierait (969519), Dunkeld (027425), Caputh (089394), Kinclaven (Isla Bridge) (163382), Stanley (119338), Luncarty (101300), Waulkmill (106290), final egress in Perth (120240).

Campsites & accommodation There are campsites at Kenmore, Aberfeldy, Grandtully, Pitlochry (off the route), Birnam, and at Perth Racecourse.

Description

Km

0   Kenmore – access on left bank.

2   Chinese Bridge. Taymouth Castle right. Right, then left after bridge.

3   Footbridge. Large island below, left channel, small islands, right channel.

4   River Lyon joins left – shingle rapid, much greater flow. This lower part of the Lyon is paddleable from below the serious stretch for some 8km from Bridge of Lyon to the confluence (see Lower Lyon).

9   Island, channel down left side but leads on to bank.

10   Aberfeldy in sight, wooded. Footpath on right bank.

10.5   General Wade's Bridge, Aberfeldy, high stone bridge. Good access and egress on right bank, parking on road. Start of 'warm-up' paddle for WW course.
Campsite on east side of town.
The river meanders around Aberfeldy, with golf course and footbridge.

12.5   Distillery and main road on right.

15.5   End of several bends in river, minor road on left bank, start of White Water Race Course - river goes right; long, bouncy rapid, large waves.

16   Edradynate access (SCA) on left bank through field, with parking. (This signed access point is some 3km upriver from Strathtay, on minor road.)
Ideal point for a trip down the WW course, through Grandtully. Several good grade 2 rapids follow.

19   Bend to left, and shallows, Grandtully comes into view, and the metal lattice road bridge can be seen. River speeds up, landing is on right side just downstream of the house and above main rapids if required. Slalom wires and poles signify start of lead-in to rapids.

19.5   Many open canoes do Grandtully (Grade 3) inspection from both banks is easy downstream of the obvious house on the right hand side, and upstream of the gabion baskets on the left. Please respect the curtilage of the house, and do not land in the garden. Except for high water, it is easiest to inspect the 'top fall' from the left bank. It is usually shot on left side, fast water to central rock, keep right, and then after bridge is the 'lower fall', which is heavy. Grandtully has multiple cafés/bars, parking at the SCA campsite, a raft operator, and plenty of activity, as it is one of the top kayaking sites in Scotland. Egress below bottom fall on the right side. If you are leaving a vehicle at Grandtully, inpection of your chosen egress before you head up the river is highly recommended.

20.5 A827 road bridge.
Islands and shallows just below, narrow channels.

25.5 Old Logierait railway bridge, now used by cyclists and walk-ers. Wood cabins for hire on left. Road to Ballinluig and A9.

27 River Tummel enters from left.
River is now near to A9 until Dunkeld.

34.5 A9 road bridge.
River through to Dunkeld very attractive, beech woods.

37.5 River Braan joins on left.

38 Dunkeld bridge. Small town, historic cathedral, shops, café, pubs, etc. Town is on the left. Left side of bridge is best, shal-low rapid below.

38.5 Birnam village is on the right bank. At sandy beach is the 'big tree' (unofficial) campsite and picnic stop, at back of housing estate.
Hills and woods close in.

47 Caputh bridge – egress on left below bridge.

50.5 River now changes character, with large shingle islands and banks, and a twisting course. Paradise for many bird species.

52 One of the largest Roman camps ever found in Scotland is 0.5km left.

56 Kinclaven bridge. Easier access and egress is at Bridge of Isla road bridge. On the left the River Isla joins just downstream. The access point is an SCA-signed one, giving easy vehicle access on to Isla, and then down 400m to the Tay, with park-ing over a field.
1km to the left is the famous Meikleour Beech Hedge, said to be the highest in the world. Go and see the plaque for the history.

57.5 Disused railway bridge.

62.5 The appearance of islands signals the top of the infamous Campsie Linn, a shock of a rapid after miles of nearly flat water. There are four shoots, with rocky and vegetated islands in between. The easiest in normal water is the second from the right, a straightforward drop. In very high water the extreme right through trees is possible. The brave might want to shoot the left route.
(For the following stretch of river, please ensure the SCA

is approached for details of what might be new physical access/egress to the Tay, due to the new Scottish Access Code, and negotiations with landowners and the local authority. This is the most heavily paddled piece of water in Scotland. It is desired not to make vehicle parking, and access to the river, a problem for local people.)

63   Burnmouth Ferry. Access on right (the Linn road from Stanley village).

63.5 Stanley Weir. Much written about over the years. Three shoots in low to medium water, middle the most water, left easiest. In high water, a strong stopper right across river. Below, a series of rapids, Catspaws and Hellhole, leading down to a bend to right. Grade 2-3. New piles of stones keep appearing in the river due to angling interests.

64   Bend to right – rapid deep on right side, shallow to left.

65   Old weir – shallows on right, wall on left, and mill leat. The leat is a beautiful paddle, newly restored in 2004, all the way down to the end of Thistlebrig Rapid. If wishing to take this, go left well up river, and keep to left bank. The leat has trees across, but is a very pleasant alternative, a good current, and is another world altogether – especially rewarding in Spring. Although the channel goes as far down as Luncarty, this is not recommended, as there are several portages past houses and sluices. Exit the leat when it starts to bend to the left, and there are obvious steps down to the river, below Thistlebrig.

On the river, the route is centre of left side. Large holes follow.

Restored Stanley Mills on right bank, belonging to Historic Scotland, well worth a visit, with café.
River bends to left.

65.5 Thistlebrig Rapid starts, (grade 3) centre over to left side, in high water right side possible.

66   Egress on right bank, but very steep walk up (the '39 Steps') to lay-by on B9099 road. Easier egress either at Luncarty or Waulkmill, further downstream.

68   Luncarty on right bank. Access through new housing estate to river, ending in a muddy path, with limited parking. (2004, turn into Poacher's Green estate, take first right, and follow this road round to left, and on to a muddy road, which eventually ends up at the river - surface due to be improved.)

69   Waulkmill on left bank. New car parking planned here (2004).

72   River Almond joins right. River becomes tidal just below here.

75   North Inch, Perth (public park) on right. Parking, landing, facilities.

75.5 Road bridge.

Firth of Tay 093

Introduction The Tay has the fastest tides of any estuary in the UK. There is absolutely no chance of paddling against it, so obtaining and understanding tide tables is paramount. Many people in small boats have drowned in or on the Tay due to not treating the river with respect, underestimating the weather and their abilities, and not planning trips properly. The tide turns on the minute that has been forecast, and the flow is obvious. The estuary is peaceful and very rural for much of the way, with rich bird life. The main channel is buoyed and lit, and small coasters still call at Perth harbour. Beware meeting them at high tide. A great trip with the tide all the way down, and a good introduction to estuary paddling.

LENGTH **38**km
OS **53/58/54**
GRADE   -

Access Access on at Perth, North Inch (120240), Inchyra (183203), Newburgh (235185), Balmerino (357249), Newport jetty (419278), egress at Tayport harbour (459290).

Campsites & accommodation Perth and Monifieth.

Description

Km

0   North Inch, followed by road bridge.

0.5   Road bridge.

1   Railway bridge – river divides, most water on right. Access probably best below here, on west (right) side alongside the South Inch.

3   Friarton Bridge, carrying the main A90 to Dundee.

6.5   Elcho Castle to R. Very old wharf and landing. Path off river.

8.5   Inchyra village left. Small jetty and landing. Sailing club. Small village.

9.5   Pylons cross, very high up. Good landmark.

11   River Earn joins right. Cairnie Pier on left bank gives egress.

12   Buoyed channel for shipping. On right bank is remains of a Roman camp, and evidence that the Romans built a pontoon bridge across the Tay at this point, only discovered fairly recently.

12.5   Mugdrum Island splits the river. Mugdrum is farmed (though flooded most winters). Farm machinery is taken over for the season by landing craft. The main channel is down right of the island, the left has more mudflats and reed banks (cultivated). The banks down the left side change each winter.

14   Newburgh on right bank. Small town with landing and very friendly sailing club. Was a port years ago.
       The estuary after this point widens out, with little habitation for quite a distance. Main channel is on the right (south) side.

16.5. Port Allan (small harbour and shelter) on left bank, hidden usually behind a reed bank.

18.5   Ballinbreich Castle on right bank.

21   Flisk Point to right – house.

26   Balmerino right – village and landing.

30   Railway bridge - Wormit village on right. Slipway after bridge.

33.5   The 'new' road bridge. Aim for arches with the navigation lights.

37   Keeping to right bank, Tayport harbour.

38   Crossing over the tideway, Broughty Ferry on left bank, landing by the castle, lowest suggested egress. Royal Tay Yacht Club on left just before Broughty Ferry.

094 Upper River Isla

LEN. **22.5**km
OS **43/44/53**
GRADE   **1-2**

Introduction The Isla is a long and shallow river, with an upper stretch which is easy for kayaks, but a bit more testing for open canoes, a very difficult section in a gorge to by-pass, and then a much flatter part as the river reaches Strathmore. The glen is an attractive one, with the Caenlochan Nature Reserve at its head, the river running off the western slopes of Glas Maol in the Glenshee ski area. This area is a good one for seeing and hearing rutting stags in the autumn. The whole of the upper glen is open, with good views. The only habitation in the glen is the tiny

Glenisla village, with a hotel of some reputation for food and good beer.

Water Level Look at rocky stretch through Glenisla village – if too dry, the river is not worth doing.

Access From the main road up Glen Isla, the B951. Access at Forter (187649), Brewlands Bridge (195615), Glenisla village (212603), egress at Bridge of Craigisla (252539).

Campsites & accommodation Nether Craig, near to egress.

Description

Km

0 In high water, the river could be done by kayak from Aucha-van, where the public road ends in the upper glen. Parking for cars, many walkers here. The valley is flat-bottomed, and the river stony and shallow. River follows the road down.

5 Little Forter bridge. Alternative start here, more water. Just above bridge is a slightly more difficult drop over rock slabs. Not much parking here.

9.5 Brewlands Bridge. Parking on grass verges. Old bridge just downstream.

11 Just when buildings in Glenisla village come into sight, the river steepens and becomes more bouldery. Easy for kayaks, more challenging for open canoes, but possible with skill. Nice stretch past the village, constant avoidance of rocks. If landing, stop at village hall and car park at top of village.

13 Old ford, former pub on left bank.

15 Road leaves river, and rapids quieten down. Isla is flat and fairly fast after this.
Two left-hand bends with easy drops, where the river appears to be girding up for more, but doesn't. River meanders.

17.5 As the river turns right, with a high slope on the left bank, rapids commence for a constant kilometre.

20 Farm bridge, woods close in on this stretch.

21 Approaching the gorge below, river drops more, with rocky rapids.

22   Old broken weir, route down left of centre. Bends.

22.5   Approaching Bridge of Craigisla, rapids under, *ensure swift exit on left, just after bridge*, onto parking area. Reekie Linn, the *highest waterfall in this part of Scotland*, is about *200m downstream*, well worth going to see.
A very deep gorge then runs southwards for 6km.

095   Lower River Isla

LEN.   **29.5**km
OS   **53**
GRADE **1-2(3)**

Portages   Ruthven Falls (grade 3) is an awkward portage and inspection, but can be carried over on right bank, left bank is private garden.

Introduction   The lower valley has Alyth and Meigle near, and the Isla joins the Tay at Kinclaven, this lower part used much for training and instruction. The first part is pleasant wooded countryside, the lower stretches have rather high banks.

Water Level   The river is mainly flat in the lower reaches. At the start, look downstream from the bridge at shallow rapids; if they are covered the river level is high enough.

Access   Airlie bridge (296505), Bridge of Ruthven, though very steep access down banks (290490), Bridge of Crathies (279455), Grange of Aberbothrie bridge (242447), Couttie's bridge (211408), and egress at Bridge of Isla (163382), which is an SCA access point.

Campsites & accommodation   Nether Craig (near Craigisla Bridge and Reekie Linn waterfall), Alyth and Blairgowrie.

Description

Km

0   Bridge over gorge on minor road from Airlie to Alyth – spectacular views and vegetation. Access is reasonably easy down steep bank on west side, downstream. Parking for only two vehicles. Small rapids.

2.5   Alyth Burn joins right. Pretty, wooded banks. River starts to steepen and narrow.

4   Mini-gorge, church high on right bank.

4.5   Ruthven bridge, egress here is awkward.
       200m further on, line of Ruthven Falls, old mill on left bank.
       The falls appear a bit more frightening than they really are, a
       line is just right of centre, heading obviously left when over
       the first drop. The falls can be inspected from the car park of
       the former tree nursery, signposted down a small road just
       west of Ruthven bridge. (Please ask, out of courtesy.)
       River now flattens out considerably, with wooded banks,
       and plenty of bird life.

6   River turns 90° to the right.

7   A line of pylons crosses the river, and 500m to the right is
       the famous 'square-top pylon', where two lines join, and
       where ospreys have nested for years. Their nest is the untidy
       jumble, totally unreachable by any predator.

8.5   The Dean Water joins from left (see Angus section). This
       stretch is often flooded way above the banks in winter.

9   Bridge of Crathies. Parking just north of bridge, also used
       by anglers.
       The next stretch is often very congested in the spring by
       trees and branches after winter floods.
       The river now winds considerably across Strathmore, and
       is an ideal piece of easy water for beginners, although not
       much scenery due to high banks.

15   Aberbothrie bridge, standing out in the flat countryside. The
       road can often be flooded in winter. Parking on verges.

17.5   River Ericht joins right (see route 097). This area appears
       isolated due to lack of roads.

22   Couttie's Bridge, Coupar Angus on obvious hill to left.
       Access on left bank, grass track up to road, with gate, park-
       ing for a maximum of three vehicles. Also used by anglers.
       Two enormous bends follow, and these open stretches often
       affected by high winds.

26   Pleasant wooded stretch to left, good stopping place.

29.5   Bridge of Isla. SCA access point on right bank, through gate
       from road (signposted). Isla shortly joins Tay, and this is the
       last egress point on Isla.

096 Upper Shee Water

LENGTH **13.5**km
OS   **43/53**
GRADE **1-2(3)**

Grade Grade 1-2, grade 3 at Blacklunans Falls (can be portaged).

Introduction These next two section are all one river. The Shee Water is formed at Spittal of Glenshee by the junction of three burns, it mysteriously morphs into the Blackwater (see Scottish White Water) at some point, and then at Bridge of Cally it is joined by the Ardle to become the Ericht, which eventually flows into the Isla.

Water Level Due to a glaciated flat-bottomed valley, the Shee Water, with a high enough flow, can be paddled by open canoe from the start. This trip does require winter high water.

Access The A93 runs south to north up the whole glen, passing through Spittal of Glenshee (111699), and Dalrulzion at the finish (136586).

Campsites & accommodation In the summer, the campsite at the finish is open. There is plenty of accommodation in the glen.

Description

Km

0   Road bridge on A93 (Blairgowrie to Braemar road, passing over Glenshee ski area).

2   Private road bridge.

3   Private road bridge.

4.5   Private road bridge - main road near.

6.5   Wooded stretch.

8.5   Cray road bridge - parking and launching alongside road below bridge.

11.5 Rocky rapids when road is alongside on left. Egress here, and fall is best inspected.

12   Large fall under Blacklunans bridge, easier in high water - aim right to avoid rocks below.

13   Three falls, or man-made weirs, heavy in high water. Back garden of hotel on main road.

13.5 Bridge into campsite. Take out below bridge on to left side (next egress is below falls).

Lower Ericht 097

Introduction A pleasant and gentle paddle through lowland scenery, to join the very meandering River Isla.

LENGTH **7.5**km
OS   **53**
GRADE   **1**

Water Level Look downstream from the bridge in the middle of Blairgowrie - the river should have an obvious route through the shallows downstream with most of the rocks covered.

Access At Blairgowrie, below the main road bridge (181450), egress off the Isla at Couttie's Bridge near to Coupar Angus (211408).

Campsites & accommodation Blairgowrie.

Description

Km

0   In Blairgowrie, take side road downstream of bridge, right side, which leads to an industrial estate. Launch from side of the road. River is at first tree-lined, with islands, and pleasant.

6   Increasingly, flood banks block out the view. Flat agricultural countryside.

7.5   Junction with River Isla.

River Earn 098

Grade Grade 1-2 mostly, some grade 3 weirs (all can be portaged).

LEN. **66.5**km
OS **51/52/58**
GRADE **1-2(3)**

Introduction The Earn is a long and possibly under-rated river, winding its way amongst various different types of scenery across the county of Perthshire. It leaves Loch Earn in the west, and at first is a tiny but interesting waterway amongst a wooded valley. At Comrie, a popular tourist village, the Earn widens out, and is nearly always canoeable from here, the trip down to Crieff, a spa town, the most popular for a day's paddle. After Crieff, the river gains in water, and has various interesting weirs down to Kinkell Bridge. Lower down, the river winds almost interminably amongst agricultural countryside, with a final tidal stretch to join the Tay.

Water Level Obvious level for paddling can be seen from bridge at Crieff.

Access The A85 follows the valley down from Loch Earn. Normal start is at power station (743225), access and egress at Comrie (775219), Crieff (857209), Kinkell Bridge (932167), Dalreoch Bridge (005179), Bridge of Earn (132187), and final egress can be at Newburgh (235186).

Campsites & accommodation Lochearnside (south side); Comrie (2 sites); Crieff (2 sites).

Description

Km

0   End of Loch Earn. High weir and sluice. River is tiny, and flows amongst many trees, with various small, stony weirs. This part requires skill from open canoeists. Can be paddled in high water, but is more reliable from Dalchonzie Power Station from which issues the piped water from Loch Earn, some 11km downstream. The main A85 road follows the river.

5.5 Power Station. Parking here (on B-road off A85), with launch over fence onto exit from power station. River is small, tree-lined and pretty.

7   Sharp bend to left, fish farm on right, long weir, shootable on left.

7.5 River bends left down a small gorge, with a rapid, and then a weir across left side of river. Passage is extreme right, with sharp bend to left at the bottom. Road on right bank.

8.5 First bridge on approach to Comrie.

9   Main road bridge in Comrie, town to left. Access/egress on right side of river downstream. Rapid under bridge, and then a grade 3 weir, which often has to be portaged on left side. Small rapids continue, with two larger ones nearer to Crieff.

14.5 Sharp bend to right in river, just before very visible monument on a hill ahead. River turns right, then left.

15   Road bridge.

18.5 Crieff road bridge - egress upstream of bridge on right side, on to land near to car park for football field. Please park with consideration. Town is up hill to left. To right is visitor centre and shopping, useful café open on Sundays, and all through winter.

23   Dornoch Mill, large weir, grade 3. Land on right side, away from house, to inspect. Can usually be shot, but tends to catch trees and rubbish.

23.5 Road bridge.

27   Colquhalzie Weir, marked by an ornamental estate bridge. Steep weir, shootable on extreme left. Has been graded 4 in past, but more likely a grade 3, regularly shot by open canoes.

27.5 First broken weir at Mills of Earn, grade 3.

28   Second broken weir, again grade 3, and shootable with care down obvious main flow.

28.5 Kinkell Bridge, the only road bridge for miles, and sign-posted from all over this part of Perthshire. Egress on left bank, with two parking areas, one by gate to estate, the other a few yards along road downstream where there is a parking area for anglers.
      The river now slows down, and meanders across its flood plain. A normal trip from here would be to Bridge of Earn, a long day's paddling.

38   Dalreoch road bridge, followed by main A9 road bridge. Access at the former.

43   Steep road bridge, Forteviot village to right. Steep wooded banks. Islands follow, and interesting oxbow lakes in this next stretch.

49.5 Railway bridge, rapid under.

51.5 Tidal limit.

52.5 Railway bridge, rapid under.

55   Bridge of Earn road bridge, village right, last egress for some miles.

55.5 M90 motorway bridge.
      The river is now still narrow, muddy and tidal, with a long sweep to the south.

63   Last possible exits from river, on to private roads on both banks, on to roads down to houses which used to be ferry points in years gone by.

63.5 Junction with the Tay estuary.

66.5 Newburgh village on right bank, egress and parking.

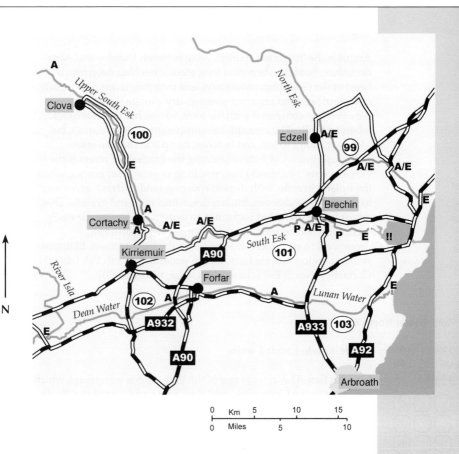

Angus

099 Lower North Esk. 166
100 Upper South Esk. 168
101 Lower South Esk. 169
102 Dean Water 171
103 Lunan Water. 172

Angus

Angus is the 'forgotten county', lying between Dundee and Aberdeenshire, but it has beautiful long glens stretching deep into the heart of the Grampian mountains, and therefore rivers. One result of eastern Scotland enjoying a sunny, dry climate is that the rivers are often low compared with the west, so one has to move quickly when rain falls. The area still has comparatively few tourists, but plenty of things to see, and beaches, camp and caravan sites.

The main geological feature affecting the gradient of rivers is the very obvious 'Highland Line', resulting in great river gorges, where the upland granite, with its peat covering (and midges), gives way to the lower sandstones, broken down into sand and gravels. This actual line, with folded rocks, not an imaginary one, can be easily seen, especially in the Gannochy Gorge of the North Esk.

From west to east, there are gorges on the Ericht (above Blairgowrie), Isla (below Reekie Linn, a high waterfall), South Esk (above Cortachy), North Esk (Gannochy Gorge, near Edzell).

099 Lower North Esk

LENGTH **13.5km**
OS **45**
GRADE **1**

Grade Grade 1 with 2 weirs.

Introduction This river is one of the long Angus waterways which rise deep in the Grampians, and flow south and east to the North Sea. The North Esk is formed from the Water of Mark and the Water of Lee above Tarfside, in bare and beautiful countryside. This section describes the North Esk from Edzell village to the sea. There is also the long 'flat' section of the river between the two difficult white water stretches, but access and egress is both difficult, and the level of this very stony stretch is rarely up high enough for a comfortable trip. If in Angus, a much better bet is the South Esk, which carries and holds more water.

If the water is reasonable, this is a nice medium grade open canoe trip.

Water Level

Judged from the start at Edzell, where there are shallow rapids, the stretch downstream should look paddleable.

Access Easiest access on to the river is from the main street in Edzell village (602689), egress at disused railway viaduct near to the sea at Montrose (725622).

Campsites & accommodation To the north, up the coast, at West Mathers and Johnshaven.

Description

Km

0   Edzell village. Access is by a track to the river and footbridge from the main street down the side of a garage. It might be easier to unload and walk the 200m or so to the river, as the track is very narrow. Parking on main street.
Launch on shallow, sandy stretch, followed by minor rapids. Pleasant wooded banks, occasional ledge rapids.

6   North Water Bridge, main A90 road to Aberdeen. Access and parking at old bridge a few metres downstream.

8.5   Railway bridge, rapid under, water goes down right side.

9   Marykirk road bridge – access and parking downstream, right side, on minor road. Usual start point for a half-day trip. Rapid on left-hand bend just below.

10.5 Logie Mill Weir (old mill is a conversion to a house, very visible on right bank). This weir has a central chute visible with retaining walls. Although looking like a minor drop, the central chute has a very powerful stopper. Shoot over left side. In flood, this whole weir disappears.

11.5 Mill of Morphie Weir. Large weir, with central fish steps. Popular fishing centre. Inspect, steps can have stoppers, but open boats usually have little problem. In high water, the weir can be shot safely down the face on the left side – often trees and branches as obstructions.
The river now has regular powerful rapids formed by rock weirs built to form fish pools.

13.5 A92 road bridge. The take-out is just below on the left, a walk through to the road to the beach, below the disused railway viaduct – parking space. This road is a very tight turn off the A92 (signposted 'Beach'), beware traffic.

100 Upper South Esk

LENGTH **18km**
OS   **44**
GRADE   **1**

Introduction The South Esk is one of eastern Scotland's best easy touring rivers, and offers one of the longest open canoe trips in the area apart from the Tay. Water and scenery differ down the valley, with this initial flat section in the upper glaciated valley contrasting with the river lower down.

Water Level Most of this stretch is flat - the upper part can be judged from the bank.

Access The B955 runs up Glen Clova, and at Gella Bridge (373653), the egress, the road splits, and both banks are followed by roads up to the Clova Hotel. From here, a single track lane leads up to Glen Doll car park (283761).

Campsites & accommodation None in the glen. Glen Clova Hotel is main accommodation around. Kirriemuir and Brechin have campsites.

Description

Km

0   Glen Doll car park. The upper river can be paddled in high water all the way from Glen Doll, at the top, and in most water from the Glen Clova Hotel, down to Gella Bridge. Council car park, rangers available, but no campsite here now. River is shallow, and often stony.

7   Clova Bridge, hotel, parking and teashop to the left. River still narrow, but it becomes slower below here. Good starting point in summer.
     River soon meanders between flat banks. In flood, river breaks banks.

18   Gella Bridge. Suggested egress. Car parks both sides. River immediately becomes bouldery, and is grade 2-3, with no easy egress for miles.

Other important points The section between the Upper and Lower South Esk is described in Scottish White Water.

Lower South Esk 101

Portages Two possible portages at weirs, one above Brechin (568587), the other at Kinnairds Mill (626583) below Brechin.

LENGTH	**38**km
OS	**54**
GRADE	**1-2**

Introduction The South Esk has dropped through a small gorge, and a very scenic 11km of constant grade 2-3 white water (a bit tight and rocky for open canoes, see Scottish White Water), and then from the start below, meanders across the plain of Strathmore. The section below Brechin is usually paddleable all year round, at least, and the river debouches into the strange tidal lagoon of Montrose Basin, a spectacular reserve for geese and wading birds.

Water Level If the upper stretches look shallow, it is worth looking lower down. The bridge at Brechin is a good place to look at the river.

Access Start either at Cortachy Bridge (395598), or Prosen Bridge (395587). Final egress at Bridge of Dun, before Montrose Basin (663585), or Montose Sailing Club (706568).

Campsites & accommodation Brechin or Forfar.

Description

Km

0   Cortachy Bridge. It is suggested that access/egress is not used here, narrow road, with verges which have been damaged in the past, and no parking. River slows down, after a considerable gorge above this point.

2   Junction with River Prosen. A normal start point, if enough water, is Prosen Bridge, 1.5km upstream (on main road up glen), easy water, and parking. Sometimes, the South Esk has plenty of water in it, but the Prosen doesn't, so it can be a frustrating bump and scrape down to the junction. From junction, fairly continuous grade 2 rapids, good test for open canoes in flood.

3.5 A sharp left-hand bend heralds a rock slab fall, followed by fast water and waves in a mini-gorge down to Shielhill Bridge. Access/egress on to old bridge, with some limited parking. Don't block entrance to house. Minor rapids follow.

5   A sharp bend to left, followed by a right bend is the beginning of a short but exciting little gorge at Castle Hill. Ahead is an obvious drop, just a rocky 1m, with a chute on left side of river. After this, two rapids with waves in a closed-in gorge. At end, a narrow gap, with swirly water. A couple more rapids.

6   Inshewan House on left bank. River now slows down for weir.

6.5   Long bend to left. Inshewan Weir has an easy concrete chute on left side, ending in islands and trees, no great difficulties.

7.5   Justinhaugh, road alongside on left, parking down near to bridge, island with fast water and a drop. Good place to judge river height; if the rapid down left side has enough water, the river will be good.

8.5   River is shallow and rocky, approaching Tannadice.

9.5   River bends to right when village appears, broken weir, covered in high water. Some limited parking, and launching, near to church in Tannadice.

11.5 Finavon bridge, main A90 road. Launching here is difficult, and there has been harassment from fishing interests in the past. (However, no places to access between here and near to Brechin. Trips will have to start either at Justinhaugh or Tannadice).

18.5 Noran Water joins from left. Gas pumping station on left bank (can be access here, but is private road). Shallows due to farm ford.

21.5 Large weir. Inspect. Shoot left side normally.

23.5 Road bridge, B-road. Egress left bank above bridge.

26   Brechin Castle estate bridge, interesting carvings on bridge.

26.5 Landing on left at Brechin car park – concrete landings, good place to start or finish trips. Rapid just downstream.

27   Road bridge – rocky slabs under.

28.5 Old weir across, left bend on to cliff, right bend down rapid. Good stopping place.

29.5 Kinnairds Mill Weir. Large weir, usual route down right side, just to right of fish steps. Rocky at bottom.
      Followed by drops which are artificial to aid salmon upstream. Popular angling spot.

32.5 Disused railway bridge, rapids.

33.5 Bridge of Dun road bridge, end of most trips. Egress on right across field, parking on bridge approaches.
River becomes tidal.

34.5 The Lurgies, mudflats on both sides, many wading birds to left.

35 Old Montrose, ancient port, on right bank. Egress and some parking, useful stopping point. Head from here directly across to sailing club, to right of obvious channel under bridge.

38 Montrose Sailing Club, egress on to ramp, and parking to side of club.

Other important points The estuary is exposed and potentially hazardous (check wind and tide).

Dean Water 102

Introduction The Dean Water is the ditch which drains Forfar Loch to the west (it is a ditch as well, a drain dug by the Glamis Estate in the 1850s, when the 'main' river, the Kerbet Burn, was straightened below Douglastown). It provides probably only a trip of local interest, but has been used to reach the sea from Forfar, the county town of Angus, via the Isla, Tay, and the sea to Arbroath, 14 miles from Forfar. The Kerbet can also be paddled in high water from some distance to the east, to make an even longer trip. The river is flat, except for two minor weirs, and a fast stretch just before the junction with the Isla.

LENGTH **17**km
OS **53/54**
GRADE **1**

Water Level The first few kilometres will be very shallow in summer, best when in near flood.

Access Access at the start from Forfar, Lochmill Farm (429498), and the A94 follows the river some distance from its left bank, access via small lanes. Egress at Crathies Bridge on the River Isla (279454).

Campsites & accommodation At Rundyhill, between Glamis and Kirriemuir.

Description

Km

0   Exit from Forfar Loch. Access is much easier, due to the A90 road culvert, at Lochmill Farm on a minor road.

0.5   Lochmill Bridge. The river is totally straight for 4km.

4   River winds through the Glamis Estate, with lovely trees, and ornamental bridges.

5.5   Road bridge, Glamis to Kirriemuir road.
River now starts to wind.

10   Small gauging weir, just before Cookston Farm bridge on a minor road.
The river now has high banks, a bit boring in low water.

11.5   River winds around a farm.

15.5   Very tight double bend, river becomes more wooded.
River is joined by the Meigle Burn, from left.
The current picks up, especially in high water. Broadleaved woodland on left.

16   Large weir, shootable on left side, and landing to inspect on grass on left side.
Converted mill on left bank follows, please do not land.
Road bridge.

17   Junction with River Isla, and egress at Crathies Bridge, right side.

103 Lunan Water

LENGTH	**9**km
OS	**54**
GRADE	**1**

Portages Could be portages required due to fallen trees, and rubble.

Introduction This is a mad, high water paddle, not known to many kayakers, and only possible when other rivers are at death height. For most of the way, an open canoe could not be turned, and there are few breakouts. The Lunan is Forfar's second river, leaving via the lochs on the east side of town.

Access From the B965, access at Boysack Mills (623491), egress at Lunan (690511).

Campsites & accommodation Carnoustie and Monifieth.

Description At Friockheim, 12km east of Forfar, two burns join, and there has been paddling from the confluence, however, with low bridges, and barbed wire. Boysack Mills has been the usual start point, and there is a constant good flow in high water, with small rapids and broken, rubbly weirs. It is about 9km down to Lunan Bay and the sea, with some surprises on the way. At The Grange, thick rhododendron almost bars the way; a knife or saw is handy. At the tidal limit, below the A92 road bridge, and the mainline railway bridge, floating bushes and rubbish often block the way, a veritable floating mat with no discernible exit. There is thick undergrowth from there down to Lunan village, a double bend, sight of a ruined castle, and the final sudden bend round to the beach. A quick exit is advised due to the surf. Exit to the beach car park is either to the left over sand dunes, or along the beach for 200m, and over the back of the beach.

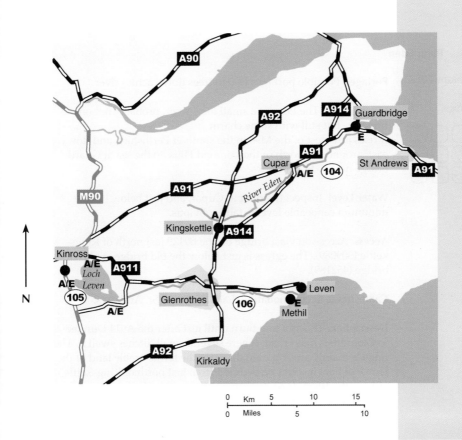

Fife

104 River Eden 176
105 Loch Leven. 181
106 River Leven 181

Fife

104 River Eden

LENGTH **20km**
OS   **59**
GRADE   **1**

Portages Possible portages due to trees down across river.

Introduction The Eden is a small local river, probably not one to travel to, but still with some charm.
It rises just west of the M90 in the south of Perthshire, and flows east, around the north of the Lomond Hills, to the sea at Guard-bridge near to St. Andrews.

Water Level Inspect the river at Cupar, and just below it – the minimum canoeable level is fairly obvious.

Access Access on via a bridge on the B9129 just north of Kings-kettle (309089). The egress is just below the old bridge at Guard-bridge (452189).

Campsites & accommodation Ladybank and St. Andrews.

Description This is a tiny burn until just after the A914 Dundee to Glenrothes main road, where several small ditches swell it. The Eden is mainly an irrigation ditch for the fertile arable land of the Howe of Fife. It could be paddled from just north of Kingskettle village, the 10km down to Cupar, but is small, shallow in summer, and is flat and straight. Near Springfield is a mill and several small weirs, likely to be shallow and rocky. A better bet is the 5km down to Dairsie Mains bridge (launch in park at Cupar, egress right side, downstream of Dairsie bridge, onto road). This stretch is in a wooded valley, with old mills, broken weirs, and often fallen trees. It is then a further 2km to the tidal limit, and 3.5km to Guardbridge. The estuary is amongst farmland, with a large caravan site on the left bank. The estuary is a Fife Council Nature Reserve, and a permit is required for this stretch.
Exit at Guardbridge on right bank onto a footpath, and then under new road bridge to old bridge a few metres downstream.

Loch Achray - www.standingwaves.co.uk

178

Forth and Clyde Canal - www.standingwaves.co.uk

Loch Lubnaig - www.standingwaves.co.uk

Falkirk Wheel - Union Canal - www.standingwaves.co.uk

Loch Leven 105

LENGTH	-
OS	58
GRADE	-

Description Loch Leven, near to Kinross and the M90, has, up to now, been barred to all water-users, and conserved for anglers (in boats with outboards), and is a major bird reserve. However, with the new Land Reform Act in Scotland, SNH are presently consulting about opening it up. Watch this space, or go and ask locally, in Perth and Kinross. It is not known where access will be, but the loch is some 13sq km in area.

River Leven 106

LENGTH	23km
OS	59
GRADE	1

Introduction This little ditch runs east from Loch Leven, through Glenrothes, 23km to the Firth of Forth between Leven and Methil, where it is industrial and polluted. Trees, weirs, sluices and rubbish bar much of the way, and it is not attractive. However, people have paddled parts of it... maybe in the future it will be cleaned up.

Access The exit from Loch Leven is at a parking place on the B9097 at the south-east corner of the loch (170993). The river becomes tidal at a bridge in Methil (375006).

River Spey - www.standingwaves.com

Central

Central

107   Balquhidder to Loch Lubnaig . 187
108   Loch Achray, Loch Venachar
        and River Teith 189
109   Loch Ard and River Forth 191
110   River Devon 193
111   River Avon 195
112   Union Canal 196
113   Forth and Clyde Canal 197

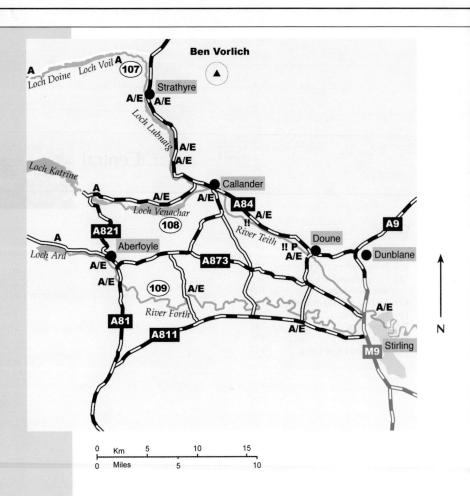

Central

107 Balquhidder to Loch Lubnaig 187
108 Loch Achray, Loch Venachar
     and River Teith 189
109 Loch Ard and River Forth . . 191

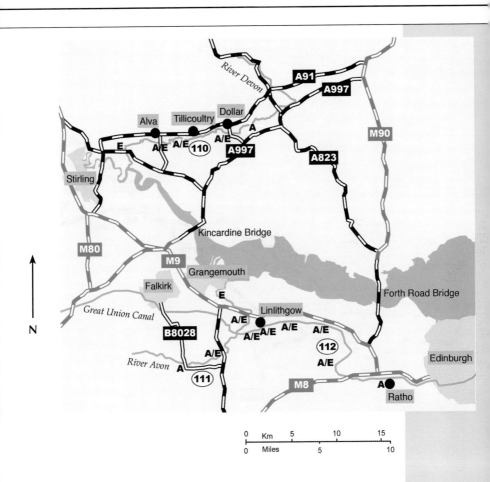

Central - continued

110 River Devon 193
111 River Avon 195
112 Union Canal. 196

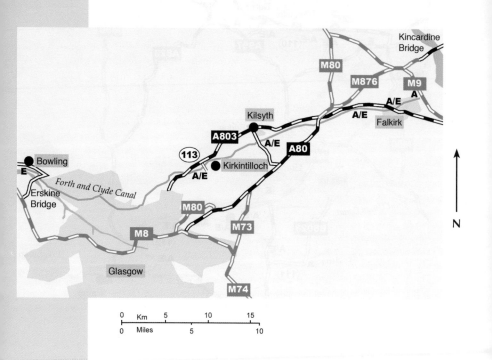

Central - continued

113 Forth and Clyde Canal 197

Central

LENGTH	**21.5**km
OS	**57**
GRADE	**1**

Outline Balquhidder, River Larig, Loch Doine, Loch Voil , River Balvaig, Loch Lubnaig.

Introduction This is an ideal beginner's trip for those not used to either paddling long distances, or canoe camping. There are no difficulties on the water, no awkward portages, there is a campsite halfway down, the trip is river and loch, and the scenery is great! The best plan is to allow two days for this; one day would be rushing too much. This area is also within easy reach of Stirling and the rest of the Central Belt.

Water Level The driest part of the Balvaig is under the bridge at the end of Loch Voil, near Balquhidder village. The level can easily be estimated from here.

Access There is only one drawback to the trip, and that is the parking of vehicles. In the whole of the glen, the road is narrow and awkward, and in order to prevent problems particular parking is referred to. It is also strongly recommended to do this trip in either spring or autumn, and avoid school holidays (Scottish and English) so as to reduce parking congestion. Many tourists come to see Rob Roy's grave in Balquhidder graveyard. If you do go there in summer, grab parking places early in the morning!
Start is on River Larig, from a passing-place (no parking)(453186). Access to Loch Voil at its eastern end at a lay-by near to the bridge over the River Balvaig (535207).
Access/egress at Strathyre campsite (558163), top end of Loch Lubnaig (564151), the first large car park on Loch Lubnaig (586118), and the last car park (585107).
Do not park in passing places on Loch Voil! Local people, especially farmers will soon move you on.

Campsites & accommodation At Strathyre.

Description The start can be on the River Larig, right up at the west end of the glen, near to the road end. The road comes near to the river about 500m before the car park at the end. Boats would

have to be off-loaded quickly to avoid congestion. The river is
slow and just wide enough for open canoes. After 1.5km, it flows
into Loch Doine (no road access), and after another 1.5km, a tiny
river of 200m or so connects this top loch with the 6km long Loch
Voil.

There are two other approaches to the trip. One is to get on somewhere along Loch Voil, but there is little parking (it would need a
drop-off in a passing place), or to park at the bottom of Loch Voil,
and paddle up. Either could give access up the connector to Loch
Doine, so they shouldn't be excluded from plans. As the tiny river
joins Loch Voil, there is a summerhouse where Buddhists from a
centre further down come to contemplate.

The south side of Loch Voil is much more peaceful to stop on,
and, approaching Balquhidder village, the River Balvaig leaves on
the right-hand side, and soon flows, fairly swiftly, under a stone
road bridge. Access is good here, with parking left side of bridge.
The river soon becomes tortuous in its bends, but there are little
rapids for the first km or so. The river then slows down, and takes
about 6.5km to reach Strathyre village on the A84 from Callander
to Crianlarich. Halfway down the minor road on the right side
of river comes close, and there is a tiny cable ferry for animals to
cross the river. The village has most facilities, the campsite being
just 200m downstream of the stone bridge (restricted parking).
Approaching the bridge, there is a small drop, either an old ford
or weir, and two rapids after the bridge.

From the campsite down to Loch Lubnaig is a good kilometre,
possible for a strong paddler to paddle back up, if the loch is
being used for a holiday.

Loch Lubnaig is a gem. It lies amongst high mountains, is 6km
long and half a km wide, and is used for Scottish sprint canoe
racing and open canoe sailing.

Just as the river flows into the loch, there is a parking place on the
left, on the main road nearby, one of three only on the loch. The
next two, which are off the road, and with picnic facilities, are a
further 4.5 and 5.5km down respectively. At the end, the River
Leny (see Scottish White Water) leaves Loch Lubnaig, and you
probably don't want to go here!

Loch Achray, Loch Venachar and River Teith

Grades Grade 1 and 2; Eas Gobhain 2-3 below bridge; Torrie rapid (3-) in high water; Deanston Weir dangerous

LENGTH**36.5**km

OS   **57**

GRADE**1/2(3-)**

Portages See text for portages on Eas Gobhain and Deanston Weir.

Introduction This trip often has to avoid the rivers above Callander due to low water levels, and results in a paddle on the River Teith from somewhere around Callander. The Teith has a deserved popularity as a beginner's white water river. The latter is also a pretty river, and an annual trip for many open boaters. The river has the quality of never being boring, having continuous small rapids, but there is only one place likely to get anything like dangerous in flood (Deanston Weir). The Callander to Deanston stretch is then grade 1 down to the junction with the Forth.

Water Level The upper connecting rivers have to be inspected. If the Teith can be launched comfortably from the car park in Callander, in other words just below the walkway, the river is a nice level.

Access Top of Loch Achray (509070), Loch Venachar off the A821 (5606), riverside car park in Callander (625069), lay-by on A84, near to Torrie Rapid (670046), below Deanston Weir (714016), final egress in Stirling on the Forth (796951).

Campsites & accommodation Callander and Cornton (Stirling).

Description

Km

0   Western end of Loch Achray – car park near to loch. Picturesque surroundings of the Trossach mountains.

2   Loch ends in the Black Water – usually enough water, a small river.

2.5   Burn enters left from the Glen Finglas reservoir.

5   River enters Loch Venachar.

7   Main road alongside on north shore – car park.

8   Loch Venachar Sailing Club on south shore, reached by a narrow road from the east only.

10   The Eas Gobhain leaves the loch, over two weirs, water-works on right bank This river is more often than not very dry, and should be inspected before paddling.

10.5 Weir.

11   Road bridge (minor road from A821 to the south side of Loch Vennacher). If the section downstream has not been inspected, land immediately after the bridge on a shingle beach on the left. Portaging over the bridge is difficult due to high stone walls. The river falls over rocky ledges, between islands and trees, for the next 300m. There is a fall of some 2m near the end of this stretch. The whole section can be portaged down the left-hand bank in a field. In low water, open canoeists can wade and line down. Kayakers will find this section straightforward in medium water. In high water, it is a serious proposition.

Access back on to the river is when buildings downstream become visible, and the river bends to the right to come nearer to the minor road down to Callander.

13   River Leny joins from left. You are virtually in Callander town now. Car park and recreation area on left bank (Meadows Car Park) which is the usual launch point.

13.5 Road bridge.

14.5 Former weir has now disappeared.

16.5 Road on right bank. Valley becomes narrower and pretty, much broadleaved woodland.

17.5 Keltie Water joins left, several bends.

19   Sharp bend to left. Torrie Rapid is a ledge run on extreme left, with a turn to right in low water to avoid undercut rock. In high water, large wave train. Two more small drops in next 400m (former slalom course).

19.5 Main A82 road on left bank. Lay-by and egress (marked by water gauge and obvious path away from river).

21.5 Private estate bridge, ornate metalwork. Former castle to left now demolished.

23   Former weir, now a noticeable rock ledge.

24   Deanston Weir. This weir is high, long, and dangerous. In low water, landing could be made on the left side of it to carry over, as the face of weir will be dry. In high water, portage

on the left side by landing about 100m above the weir, on to a track high up on the left bank, and get back in down stone steps below the weir. An alternative could be lining down the fish steps on the right side, but landing at the sluices, and carrying over, is difficult. The steps are easier for kayaks. The face of the weir has a 1m drop at the end, and a substantial stopper in high water. Egress to Deanston from here is difficult (fence with barbed wire).

24.5   Take out right side just after sewage works, up over wire gabions, to Deanston village. There is good parking space here by the gates of the sewage works.

25   A84 road bridge.

26.5   Weir. River now widens, slows down – several islands.

32   River Forth joins on the right. The Teith often carries more water than the Forth.

33   M9 road bridge. Just below, a shallow weir (covered at some high tides). Upper tidal limit. Rapids below at some states of tide.

34   Allan Water joins left.

35.5   Campsite on left bank, and egress.

36.5   Stirling bridge (old bridge, followed by modern road bridge). Egress recommended to left of old bridge, now pedestrianised. River below has very muddy banks.

Loch Ard and River Forth 109

Introduction The Forth sounds like a major river, with a giant estuary, but is a disappointment. It's usually easy to say something good about Scottish rivers, but the Forth is … boring. It is a very long, narrow, winding river for most of its length, with very restricted views due to high banks. Many open canoeists do it to say they've done it, and then wonder why!

LENGTH	56km
OS	57
GRADE	1

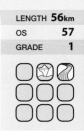

Water Level The level of the river running through Aberfoyle is a good indicator of the higher stretch – a scrape, and it will be a pain, although most of the Forth downstream will be alright, as it is like a canal.

Access Loch Ard (4502), north side off B829, Aberfoyle bridge (520010), Shannochill campsite (532989), south of Aberfoyle,

Dykehead bridge on B8034 (599973), B822 bridge (668960), Gargunnock bridge B8075 (715952), and egress either at Craigforth, before Stirling (770956) at the old bridge, or in Stirling.

Campsites & accommodation Shannochill, Thornhill or Stirling.

Description The start up at Loch Ard is pretty and the paddle to Aberfoyle rewarding, with wooded banks. If you insist on doing it, rough camping is quite possible, but not very attractive. Escape to the Stirlingshire villages to the south brings some nice pubs, if you're stuck. The flatness of the landscape is due to the river passing through Flanders Moss, one of the last raised bogs in central Scotland. Canoe campers have been known to have fled screaming after a couple of days of this paddling, especially if they are joined by midges in the summer.

Km

0   Kinlochard village on Loch Ard. Parking and landing/access. The loch is some 3km long, with wooded banks, a crannog and a castle, well worth exploring.

3   Exit to the Forth is in the south-east corner, quite narrow and hidden.

4   The loch/river narrows at Milton village, to left.
       Duchray Water joins right (see Scottish White Water).

5.5   Aberfoyle bridge, village left. All services and shops.

8.5   A wooded stretch ends at the A81 (Glasgow road) bridge. The nice scenery now ends, and the river enters a dark green mass of plantations soon after this. Gartrenich Moss to left, Flanders Moss to right.

12.5   Kelty Water joins right.

21   Road bridge. Port of Menteith 4km left, Arnprior 2.5km to the right.

24.5   Farm bridge.

31   B822 road bridge. Kippen 2km to right. The river winds even more now.

42   B8075 road bridge.

56   A84 road bridge. The River Teith joins from left, often with more flow. It is now a further 4.5km down to Stirling bridge.

River Devon (Clackmannanshire) 111

Portages Possible portage before Dollarfield.

LENGTH	**19**km
OS	**58**
GRADE	**1**

Introduction The Devon is a delightful and pretty river which rises in Perthshire, and then flows along the border between Kinross and Clackmannanshire, most of its course being within the latter's borders, before it joins the Forth just downstream of Stirling. It rises west of the Upper and Lower Glendevon reservoirs in a remote part of the Ochil Hills, flows east then south down a typical glen, and is first seen by many people as it flows under the A91. Don't be misled, however, as although in high water the river could be paddled from here, the Devon becomes smaller, drier and much overgrown near Crook of Devon (3km down). The valley then turns west, and just before the A823 at Rumbling Bridge (a clue here), it plunges into a deep gorge. Looking at the countryside, this is quite unexpected, and the river is some 30 to 40m down. Exploration of the valley below here is very difficult, although the map marks a waterfall a further 2km downriver.

When Vicar's Bridge is reached, the next road bridge, life becomes easier, and the Devon is in its final lowland stages. Distances are given from here.

Water Level Looking downstream from the start point at Vicar's Bridge, the little shallow rapids should be able to float a canoe.

Access Vicar's Bridge, on minor roads between the A91 and A977 (986980); Dollarfield bridge, near Dollar (961970); Glenfoot bridge, below Tillicoultry (910964); Alva bridge (884962); egress at A907 bridge, west of Tullibody (846952).

Campsites & accommodation At Dollarfield bridge.

Description

Km

0   Vicar's Bridge. Good parking here. Bridge reached by a very small, single-track and wooded lane from either the A91 to the north, or the A977 to the south. If looking downriver, there are obvious shallows, the river will be a pain down to Dollar. River pretty, very wooded, with trees across in

places. In high summer, the banks are covered with the pink of Indian Balsam and wild garlic.

2.5   Small weir – can be easily carried round on right side, camp-site.

3.0   Dollarfield bridge, and camp and caravan site on north (left) bank. Owners welcoming to those wishing to park cars. The first 2km or so of river from here are very winding and wooded, with frequent possible obstructions (not the straight river as shown on OS maps).

5.0   Footbridge – slightly deeper water from now on.

5.5   First of four sheep fences – this one has to be carried over.

6.0   Footbridge, followed by shingle bank on right bank, and egress to main road at lay-by.

River becomes much more sandy and shingle. Area on left bank of old oxbow lakes. Second sheep fence.

7.0   Main road near again on right bank. Many sharp bends.

7.5   Old rail bridge, now a footbridge. Tillicoultry is now near on right bank, but little sign. First sign is a furniture store car park on right.

8.5   Tillicoultry road bridge – poor access, better to paddle on to Glenfoot bridge.

River is still rural in appearance, old industrial signs.

9.5   Glenfoot bridge, egress right bank, upstream, car parking on waste land just over minor road.

12.5   Road bridge. Alva to right, Fishcross left.

13.5   Alva road bridge. Narrow road, some parking on waste ground to right.

17.5   Menstrie road bridge, no parking.

18   Old rail bridge.

19   A907 road bridge. Last chance to leave river, 2km before it joins a very muddy Forth. Access/egress on old bridge, possible parking on old road.

River Avon (West Lothian) 111

Distances 15km (usually 10km in low water).

Grades Grade 1-2 (top 5km) and grade 2-3 (lower 10km).

LENGTH **15km**
OS   **65**
GRADE**1-2/2-3**

Introduction The Avon is a short rural delight near to industry. It rises in the hills to the south of Falkirk, and could be paddled the 5km down from Avonbridge when high, (when the lower half is considerably more difficult). The next 6km is the best part, running through a wooded gorge. From Linlithgow down is a rather industrialised 4km, with egress just before the river becomes tidal approaching the oil and chemical complex of Grangemouth.

Water Level A look over at Avon Gorge will soon tell you if there is enough water in the small rapids, or a look over the high banks within Muiravonside Country Park.

Access At Avonbridge on the B8028 at the top (911728), Avon Gorge bridge (park with care, dangerous road) 955736); Linlithgow (983773), and final egress at Polmonthill (949796).

Campsites & accommodation Linlithgow.

Description There is little road access to the higher part, so trees across could make passage quite difficult, so beware. The river can be seen at Strath House, halfway down, but narrow country lanes, and no parking. Grade 1-2.
The lower 6km from the A801 Avon Gorge road down to Linlithgow is either a rocky grade 2 in medium water, or grade 2-3, with some interesting and testing rapids in a wooded gorge. Most of this passes through Muiravonside Country Park (Falkirk Council), a delightful valley with active badger setts. If in doubt, go in and talk to the Rangers, and you can prospect much of it. After the park, the river passes under the aqueduct for the Union Canal. For this lower stretch, park carefully, probably not right on the bridge, which is restricted. Take out just after the road bridge and weir coming into Linlithgow. (This is Linlithgow Bridge, and has a pub on it).
Below here is industrial and canalised, but the rather smelly river runs for another 4km until just before it becomes tidal.

112 Union Canal (Edinburgh to Falkirk)

LENGTH **50km**

OS   **65/66**

GRADE   -

Introduction Ensure that you have the most up-to-date OS maps, as both the Union and Forth and Clyde canals have received a great injection of cash from the Millennium Fund around the turn of the last century, and this has resulted in former dry stretches being renovated, and a large new length of canal being dug around Falkirk. In addition, the Falkirk Wheel, truly one of the engineering wonders of the modern world, has been constructed to lower boats 35m down to the Forth and Clyde, which replaces 11 locks, the largest rotating boat lift in the world.
For full details, see www.thefalkirkwheel.co.uk.

Access For the current access point at the east end, in west Edinburgh, see the British waterways website www.scottishcanals.com seasonal differences.
Useful access points at Ratho village, by the pub (139708); Broxburn, Winchburgh, Fawnspark on the B8046, near to the M9 (060768); Philipstoun, path by the bridge (041771), Linlithgow, and the Falkirk Wheel (853801).

Campsites & accommodation No formal sites anywhere near to the canal, as this is a mainly former industrial area. Sites back in Edinburgh, and at Cuthill, near West Calder.

Description The Union Canal runs for 50km from the west side of Edinburgh to Falkirk, following the contours of the West Lothian countryside, with spectacular aqueducts at Slateford in Edinburgh, the Edinburgh by-pass, and the river valleys of the Almond and Avon. It winds around Ratho, under the M8, Broxburn, Winchburgh, through the middle of Linlithgow, and is now routed around the back of the town of Falkirk. It then passes in a new tunnel under the Roman Antonine Wall, before bursting out on a high level with a great view to the north, over the Wheel Basin.

Other important points For full details of bridges, locks and operational requirements see www.scottishcanals.com.
At the Falkirk Wheel, paddlers will be pleased to know that they can merely walk down the grassy bank to join the canal heading westward.

Forth and Clyde Canal 113

Portages Portages around locks, which are in about 6 clusters.

LENGTH **56km**

OS   **64/65**

GRADE   -

Introduction This canal has also had bridges raised in height, and has been cleaned up, making it now 56km from its basin just east of the Union Canal on the tidal River Carron, to Bowling on the Clyde.

Access East to west, Carron basin (905822), near to the M9 at Falkirk; the Falkirk Wheel basin (853801); various places on the banks west of Bonnybridge (8179); west of Kilsyth, off the B8023 (7076); Glasgow Bridge (parking place), west of Kirkintilloch on the A803 (634730); various road bridges through Glasgow, but none specially recommended; and then Bowling Basin at the western end (450736).

Campsites & accommodation None on the canal (see the cross-country route for advice on rough sites); nearest sites at Strathclyde Park, south of Glasgow, or on Loch Lomond.

Description There are 39 locks, 20 on the west side, 19 on the east, plus bridges which are raised. For up-to-date details see www.scottishcanals.com.

The most pleasant parts of the canal scenically are the east and central parts. Falkirk has been 'cleaned up' and much revitalised with the impact of the Falkirk Wheel, and there are now canalside pubs and gardens where once there was industry.

Leaving Falkirk, the canal passes under the Wheel basin, and then follows the line of the Antonine Wall (due for renovation itself in the future), the Bonny Valley up to the watershed about where the M80 passes over, and then the pastoral Kelvin Valley towards Glasgow.

The Glasgow section is usually described as not so pleasant, as the canal winds its way through the northern and western suburbs, but new developments are taking place all the time. On Clydebank, people are taking an interest in the canal as it provides their riverside corridor between themselves and the Clyde.

The end at Bowling tends to be muddy and industrial. The Erskine Bridge is just upstream of this point, Dumbarton a few kilometres downstream.

Both of these canals have been paddled in a (long) day, but if camping, the Forth and Clyde has possible rough campsites near Kilsyth, and the Union Canal near to the Avon Gorge, or Winchburgh.

South

South

Ayrshire
114 River Ayr 201
115 Loch Doon. 203
116 River Doon 203

The Clyde Valley
117 Upper Clyde 206
118 Lower Clyde. 207

Dumfries and Galloway
119 Luce Bay 211
120 Isle of Whithorn and Garlieston 211
121 Gatehouse of Fleet. 212
122 Brighouse Bay, Kirkcudbright Bay 212
123 Rivers Ken, Dee and Loch Ken 217
124 Auchencairn Bay, Orchardton
     Bay and Rough Firth. 219
125 Lower Nith and Nith Estuary . 220
126 River Annan. 221

Borders
127 River Tweed. 225
128 River Teviot 229

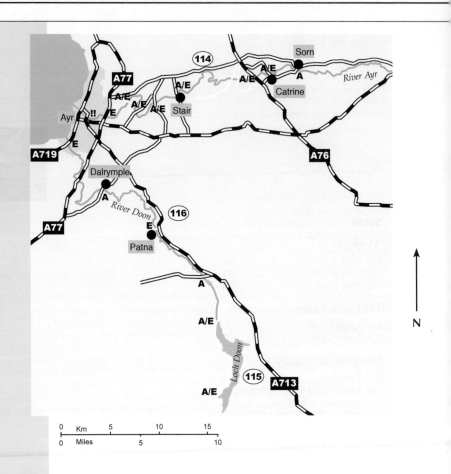

Ayrshire

114 River Ayr 201
115 Loch Doon. 203
116 River Doon. 203

Ayrshire and Lanarkshire

The two Ayrshire rivers below both appear in 'Scottish White Water', as easier rivers than the norm in the guide. A brief account of distances is given below to aid paddlers, but both require water to make them a reasonable prospect to paddle, and therefore travel any distance.

River Ayr 114

LEN.	**41.5**km
OS	**70/71**
GRD.	**1/2(3)(4)**

Portages Portages can be made at the weir at Catrine (grade 4), and Auchincrave (grade 3).

Introduction The Ayr is a long river, rising on the Lanarkshire/Ayrshire border, and flowing west for some 50km to the sea at Ayr. It is a good river for paddlers to become used to easy rapids (the bedrock is 'soft' sandstone), and the hazards can be portaged. A possible open canoe trip. The countryside is bare higher up, becoming wooded and attractive in the lower reaches. Grade 1/2, apart from hazards mentioned below. Many of the road bridges are high above the river valley, so inspect for access and egress points.

Water Level Look over any of the bridges at sandstone shallows. The paddling level is obvious.

Access Sorn bridge (555265), Catrine bridge (530259), old bridge off A76 (516253), Stair bridge (438235), Annbank bridge (413227), Tarholm bridge (393221), Auchencruive bridge (388231) and A77 bridge (363216).

Campsites & accommodation
Coylton, on the River Coyle, Crofthead, near Ayr, and Cumnock. Ayr is very much an old mining county, especially inland from the sea. A stay might be more pleasant in one of the seaside campsites south of Ayr in the Culzean area.

Description
Km

0   Sorn village. The river higher up has waterfalls in a forest area. Parking upstream of bridge, on right side of river.

Immediately, the river bends sharply right, then left. Weir of 2m drop just around corner, inspect from left, gentle slide.

2.5   Double weirs (grade 4). Portage.

3.5   Catrine village, road bridge. Access/egress at bridge is quite difficult, as it is in the middle of the village. 200m downstream, access is much easier on right side at recreation park, parking over grass on the road.
Steep wooded valley, in next 4km, three road bridges and railway bridge.

8   Lugar Water joins on left. Weir. Road bridge, Mauchline 2km on right.

9   Barskimming bridge – easier access and egress.
Warning: The next 9.5km is a grade 2/3 stretch through an attractive wooded gorge, with no great difficulty. Possible escape at Failford halfway down, on right bank. In high water, the weir just above Stair has a large wave on it.

18.5 Stair village. Access/egress at road bridge (B730).

21.5 Road bridge. Annbank village to right. Old railway bridge just before it.

25   Water of Coyle joins on left.

25.5 Road bridge. Tarholm to right.

32.5 Road bridge. Auchincruive Agricultural College to right. Rapid/broken weir at bridge could be grade 3.

36.5 Main road bridge, Ayr by-pass, (A77). Egress not easy, but perhaps a better finish point than in Ayr, where there is a dangerous weir in high water, just before the first road bridge (5km further on).

Loch Doon 115

Distances Round trip of 16km.

LENGTH	**16km**
OS	**77**
GRADE	-

Introduction Loch Doon is hidden away high up in the trees of the Carrick Forest, but near to the main A713 road, from Galloway to Ayr. It is reached by a minor road which leaves the A713 2km south of Dalmellington, and joins the loch at the north end where the River Doon exits.

Access At north end (476014), off the road which follows the west bank, or at the southern end at Craigmalloch (483949). After this point, the road becomes a forest drive (toll road) heading west through the Carrick Forest.

Campsites & accommodation No formal sites, wild camping in the forest.

Description The loch is almost Canadian in nature, being surrounded by conifers, and is only about 0.5km wide, and could provide entertainment for half a day.

River Doon 116

Distances 7km and 10km.

LENGTH	**17km**
OS	**70**
GRADE	**1/2**

Introduction Two separate lengths of river, missing out a 10km stretch in the middle, offering a useful trip if in the area.

Water Level Easily surmised at the various bridges by looking at the small rapids.

Access B741 bridge, near to Dalmellington (462060), down to Patna bridge (417106). The second stretch is from Dalrymple bridge (359144) to the A719 bridge (326190) near to Ayr, with access/egress also at Auchendrane bridge (335155).

Campsites & accommodation Around Ayr.

Description The river is grade 1 or 2 for most of its length. The upper stretch of 3.5km (from the Loch Doon dam) down to

Bogton Loch is grade 3, but the further 8km down to Patna (egress at road bridge over river) is grade 1. Then follows a more difficult part of 10km to Dalrymple, grade 2/3, but grade 3+ in high water. After this, 6km of flatter water follow to Auchendrane on the A77 (limited parking), then the final section to Doonfoot near Ayr is 4km of grade 2, with small weirs, fishing platforms, and anglers. The river is wooded and pretty for much of the way.

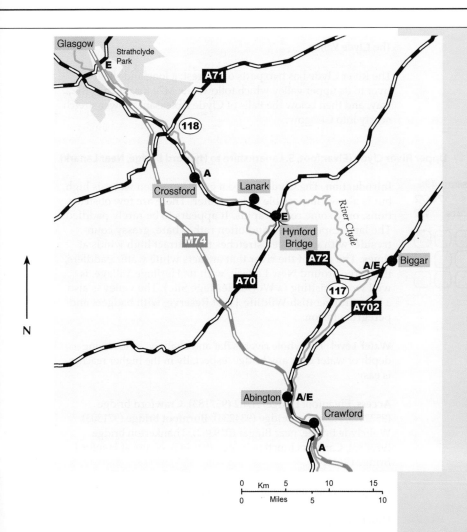

The Clyde Valley

117 Upper Clyde. 206
118 Lower Clyde. 207

The Clyde Valley

The River Clyde has two parts of interest: a long and shallow river in its upper valley which follows the M74 for much of the way, and then below the Falls of Clyde a pleasant, slower stretch nearly into Glasgow.

117 Upper River Clyde (Elvanfoot, S. Lanarkshire to Hynford Bridge, Near Lanark)

LENGTH **49**km
OS   **78/72**
GRADE   **1/2**

Introduction The Clyde can be a good bet when water is high, but is almost impossible in low water. There are few obstructions, only some rocky rapids. It appears to be rarely paddled. The landscape is open, and often rather bare, grassy countryside, with wide open stretches that attract high winds at times. The part of the river that attracts white water paddlers, the gorge around New Lanark, with its Heritage Village, is well worth visiting (a World Heritage Site). The valley is also a beautiful Scottish Wildlife Trust Reserve, with badgers and peregrine falcon.

Water Level The whole river is flat and shallow, so assessing depth of water over any bridge, especially in the higher reaches, is easy.

Access Elvanfoot bridge, A702 (957183), Crawford bridge (952212), Abington bridge (934234), Burnfoot bridge (971303), Wolfclyde bridge, near Biggar (019362), Thankerton bridge (978383), Carstairs Junction bridge (956445), egress at Hynford Bridge (914414).

Campsites & accommodation Moffat, Crawford and Lanark.

Description

Km

0   Elvanfoot, just downstream from the joining of various burns, and the Daer reservoir, which supplies most of the water. Access at the old road bridge near to (east of) the motorway M74.

4.5   Road bridge, and Crawford village to left. Ruined castle on right.

9   Road bridge. Abington village to left. The river now turns
      north-east and flows down near to Biggar, one of the few
      towns on the whole route.

12   Duneaton Water joins left.

13   A702 road bridge. The scenery is now dominated by Tinto
      Hill (702m) to the north.

18.5 Road bridge. Lamington village to right.

26.5 A72 road bridge. Biggar town 2km to right. River now
      widens and slows down.

31.5 Road bridge. Thankerton village to left. River now meanders
      over a very flat plain.

40   Road bridge. Carstairs Junction (a central rail junction for
      Scotland) to right.

48.5 Hynford Bridge. Egress advised here, as Bonnington Linn (a
      major waterfall) is next feature, some 4km downstream. The
      river now changes character dramatically, to a steep-sided
      wooded valley. Lanark 4km right.

Lower River Clyde (Crossford to Strathclyde Country Park) 118

Grade Grade 1 (Garrion Weir at 794509, which is harder in high
water), grade 2 at Crossford.

LENGTH	**18**km
OS	**72/64**
GRADE	**1(2)**

Portages Garrion Weir can be portaged on both banks.

Introduction A useful paddle near to Glasgow in countryside.

Water Level Most of the river is slow and deep, and the Clyde
down here keeps its level for a long time after rain. A look at
Crossford will tell the paddler the level.

Access Crossford village, left bank downstream of bridge
(827465). Garrion Weir bridge, downstream of bridge, reached by
taking a dead end down to nursery / garden centre and parking in
cul-de-sac next to roundabout up on main road (793511). Strathclyde Park Watersports Centre (730565), egress at Strathclyde Park
Visitor Centre (719579).

Campsites & accommodation Lanark and Strathclyde Park.

Description

Km

0   Crossford village is some 6km downstream from Lanark.
Good access on left. below bridge, which has a rock shelf
under it. (The water just upstream is nice, grade 2, but access
is difficult). The countryside is pretty, with much of the
Clyde Valley's soft fruit industry here, in many glasshouses.

3   Main road, A72 on left bank.

6.5   Garrion Weir – usually the lip is blocked by trees and rubbish. Ramp on extreme right, easy shoot in moderate water.
Road bridge.

15.5   River Avon joins left, followed by road bridge (A723).
Entrance to Strathclyde Park, (loch just over bank on right side).
Water Centre on right bank. Egress either here, or...

18   Egress near to Visitor Centre, on to path on right bank. From
here on, the river becomes more industrial, and egress is
often difficult. Also, some large weirs.

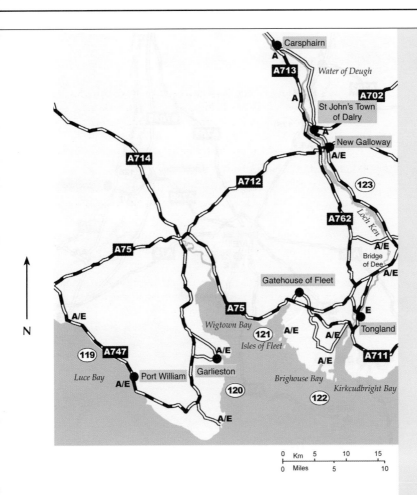

Dumfries and Galloway

119 Luce Bay 211
120 Isle of Whithorn and Garlieston 211
121 Gatehouse of Fleet 212
122 Brighouse Bay, Kirkcudbright
    Bay. 212
123 Rivers Ken, Dee and Loch Ken. 217

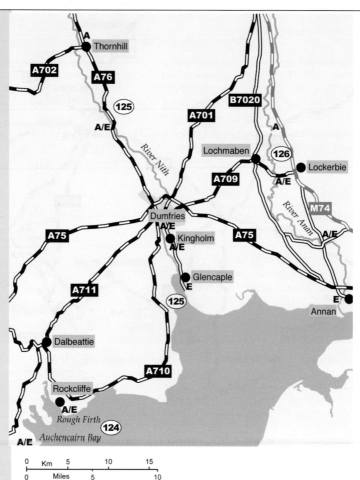

Dumfries and Galloway continued

124 Auchencairn Bay, Orchardton
     Bay and Rough Firth 219
125 Lower Nith and Nith Estuary . 220
126 River Anan 221

Dumfries and Galloway

This whole coast is known for fast tides, sandbanks, and exposed headlands. Short trips are possible in many of the sheltered bays. The main rivers offering any distance for paddling are the Ken/ Dee, Nith and Annan. Other rivers are mainly very shallow unless in high flood. The whole area however is a delight for tourists, with an attractive coast, small villages and great stretches of forest with many walks.

Luce Bay 119

Campsites & accommodation Glenluce and Auchenmalg Bay.

Description There are not many possibilities in this bay, most of it being an RAF bombing range. A coastal trip from Glenluce down to Port William is a possible safe trip in good weather (21km), but further down nearer to Burrow Head is exposed.

LENGTH	-
OS	**82**
GRADE	-

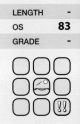

Isle of Whithorn and Garlieston 120

Campsites & accommodation Wigtown.

Description 12km between these two points. Isle of Whithorn is a picturesque sailing centre. Further in to Wigtown Bay exposes very large areas of sand and mud at low tide.

LENGTH	-
OS	**83**
GRADE	-

121 Gatehouse of Fleet

LENGTH **12**km
OS   **83**
GRADE   -

Campsites & accommodation Gatehouse of Fleet, Brighouse Bay, and various small caravan sites and informal/seasonal sites.

Description A scenic bay of some 12km coastline in all, out to the Islands of Fleet to the south, well worthwhile exploring, with the right tide (maybe last of the flood, start of ebb), and landing at one of the bays south of the southernmost island, Barlocco Isle. Airds Bay, on the south side of Fleet Bay has landing, a road, and a caravan site.

122 Brighouse Bay, Little Ross and Kirkcudbright Bay

LENGTH **18**km
OS   **83**
GRADE   -

Distances Round trips of 8km and 18km.

Introduction This area is well known to paddlers, offering interesting possibilities for trips, especially sheltered waters for beginners, and some more challenging voyages if wished. Brighouse Bay is a long-established camp and caravan site, with a beach fronting it, ideal for learning surfing.

Access From Brighouse Bay beach (636458).

Campsites & accommodation Brighouse Bay, and Kirkcudbright.

Description A trip round to Little Ross, at the mouth of Kirkcudbright Bay, can be either very straightforward, or a problem if wind gets up. The 5km paddle in to Gull Craig is a common trip, again further in to the bay being awkward with the large expanse of tidal mud.

Starting the run down the fish-ladder - River Teith - Karen Macneish

Who put that log there? - River Teith - Karen Macneish

Keep the upstream gunwhale up! - River Teith - Karen Macneish

They're off again - River Teith - Karen Macneish

... and they've made it! - River Teith - Karen Macneish

Regrouping at the portage - River Teith - Karen Macneish

Rivers Ken, Dee and Loch Ken 123

Grade Grade 1 and 2, but Water of Deugh grade 2-3, and Earlstoun Linn 2/3.

LENGTH **48**km
OS **77/83**
GRADE**1/2(2/3)**

Portages Several portages at dams, and sometimes over dry sections of river, see text.

Introduction This is still a relatively little-visited area of Scotland, and offers peace and quiet and plenty of wildlife. The river and loch system offers many different types of paddling, with some awkward portages as well, due to the connected and complicated hydro-electric system. Turbines running usually mean water below the dams, and often in the middle of the day (apparently!). A trip could be started, if there is water, as high up as Carsphairn, but often paddling has to commence at Carsfad Loch.
There are some rocky rapids below dams, and a grade 2/3 fall at Earlstoun Linn, above Earlstoun Loch. The river sections are generally grade 2. More suitable for an open canoe trip below Allangibbon bridge, near St. John's Town of Dalry.
It is suggested that, if camping, you stay on Loch Ken and do the river in two days.

Water Level Paddlers have to go and look! Loch Ken and River Dee will always have enough water.

Access Carsphairn bridge (568930), Kendoon (601878), below Carsfad Loch dam (604854), Allangibbon bridge (615820), Ken bridge (New Galloway) (640784), Loch Ken viaduct (684703), Crossmichael (7267), Glenlochar dam (732644), Bridge of Dee (734600), egress before Tongland dam (703550).

Campsites & accommodation Loch Ken, east side, just south of Loch Ken Viaduct, and Kirkcudbright.

Description
Km

0   Carsphairn. Bridge over Water of Deugh (A713).
     This first stretch is a rocky grade 2/3, not easy at all for open canoes.

3   Kendoon Loch.

5   Bridge over loch, halfway down. Fish farm below bridge. Dam and outflow below to right, portage to river, which may be dry. Carrying on leads to another dam in 1.5km and Gleghoul Glen ,which might well also be dry! *Inspect all sections below dams in advance.*

7.5   Kendoon Power Station, where the two rivers join. You are now properly on the Water of Ken. Car parking probably best at Polmeddie FC car park west of road.

8.5   Carsfad Loch.

10   End of loch, dam, portage right. Water of Ken river, rapids. Lay-by on main road below dam, very convenient for rapids.

11   Just after the Polharrow Burn joins from right, river bends left, then right, Earlstoun Linn, a two-step fall, possible with care for open canoes. Take care below, as fast water follows, and a possible 3m fall if loch below is dry.

11.5   Earlstoun Loch.

13   End of loch, dam, long portage right.

14   Allangibbon bridge. St. John's Town of Dalry to left. Small market town.
       Water of Ken is now a broad river with good water. Anglers often found on this stretch. River is always paddleable below here.

20   Bridge of Ken. New Galloway 1km to right. The A713 is now on right bank all the way down Loch Ken. Scenery changes from upland wooded hills to more open agricultural land.

22   River becomes Loch Ken, almost imperceptibly. Kenmure Castle on right bank.

25.5   Loch Ken Sailing Centre on left bank. Canoes and dinghies for hire, instruction, café. This upper part of the loch is ideal for canoe sailing.
       Islands follow.

29.5   Ken Viaduct (disused railway line, now footpath). Power boats on this stretch, with water-skiing.

30   Campsite on left bank. Black Water of Dee joins right.
       Loch is now interesting, with islands, shallows and narrows. Flatter, more open scenery.

33.5   Narrows. Islands with many wading birds.

35   Crossmichael village on left bank.

37.5 Glenlochar Dam. Lift over into River Dee.
      Wide, deep river. No rapids.

40   Threave Island. Right channel is smaller, but passes Threave
      Castle. Rapid where two channels rejoin.

41   Lodge Island.

41.5 Old railway bridge, followed by main road. Threave bridge
      A75, town of Castle Douglas 4km left.
      Rapid starts under bridge for 100m.

42   Bridge of Dee. River quietens down, islands, river becomes
      Tongland Loch.

48   Land on right side of loch at lay-by on road, before Tongland
      Dam, where egress is awkward.

Auchencairn Bay, Orchardton Bay and Rough Firth 124

Distances Round trip of 14km from Rockcliffe to Auchencairn via Hestab Island.

Campsites & accommodation Rockcliffe, Kirkcudbright, and Southerness.

Description Again possibilities for the paddler, but only near to high tide. Kippford in Rough Firth is a major sailing centre, and is very sheltered.

LENGTH **14km**

OS   **84**

GRADE   -

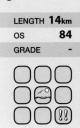

125 Lower Nith and Nith Estuary

LEN.	**34.5**km
OS	**78/84**
GRADE	**1-2**

Introduction The Nith is rather a strange river. It rises in Ayrshire, between Dalmellington and New Cumnock, where several burns leave a flat, wooded area that has been an opencast coal mine, then flows eastwards through flat, bleak and rather featureless countryside. It could be paddled from New Cumnock; to Kirkconnel is 15km, and a further 6.5km to Sanquhar (a former fireworks manufacturing town), where the Nith turns southwards. It is flat and winding. Then at Mennock, 4km downstream, the river changes in character and becomes a white water river for 11km. (See Scottish White Water).

The lower, pleasant agricultural section is usually paddled from Thornhill, giving 27km, a long day trip down to Dumfries, with the possibility of extending the trip further down the estuary.

Water Level Fairly obvious from bridges, especially from new Dumfries by-pass bridges.

Access Thornhill bridge (871955), Auldgirth old bridge (912864), Dumfries bridge above weir (967761), Kingholm Quay (975736) and Glencaple (994685).

Campsites & accommodation Penpont, near Thornhill, east of Dumfries on A75.

Description

Km

0   Thornhill bridge. Town to left.

4.5   Scar Water joins left. Rapids.

10.5   Barburgh Mill and main road (A76) to left.

12.5   Auldgirth bridge.

17   Old railway bridge, weir under, probably portage left.

24   First of new by-pass bridges.

24.5   Old railway bridge, said to have metal spikes on it. Outskirts of Dumfries.

       Second new by-pass bridge.

25   Third new bridge, followed by old railway bridge.

27   Dumfries town bridge, followed by a two-step weir with
      fish-run down left bank. Big in flood.

      River becomes tidal.

29.5 Kingholm Quay left. Old port for Dumfries, with warehouses.

34.5 Glencaple village left. Useful egress point.
      The river then widens out considerably into the Solway
      Firth. The Caerlaverock Nature Reserve on the left side (east)
      is well worth a visit.

River Annan 126

Grade Grade 1 and 2. Four weirs.

LENGTH	**30km**
OS	**78/85**
GRADE	**1/2**

Introduction The Annan is a long, pastoral river of some 30km,
flowing through the eastern part of Dumfries-shire, now known
better to travellers to Scotland as the M74 corridor. The countryside is quiet rather than especially beautiful, but with water in it
the Annan would provide a day's easy paddling as an alternative
to the English Lakes or the Solway coast.
It rises in the hills above Moffat, in the spectacular box canyon
known as the Devil's Beeftub, is tiny through the town of Moffat,
and is usually seen first by travellers at the Johnstonebridge Services on the M74, where it curls around the artificial ponds. The
river can be paddled in high enough water from just below the
service station, a kilometre or so down the lane on the west side of
the river. Distances are given, however, from the next road bridge
some 8km down, as the Annan is joined soon after by Water of
Ae which nearly doubles its size. Many of the bridges have little
parking, so vehicles should be left with care.

Water Level A look over bridges will soon tell you if the river
has water.

Access Millhousebridge (103855), A709 bridge (106807), minor
road bridge (118761), Hoddom bridge (163728), Brydekirk bridge
(187705) and Annan bridge (191665).

Campsites & accommodation Lochmaben, Hoddom Castle and
Annan (near to finish).

Description

Km

0   Millhousebridge, 1km west of the M74.

1.5   Applegarthtown village left bank. Ancient motte.

2   Water of Ae joins right.

4.5   River has many bends, a lagoon to right fast becoming an oxbow lake. Dryfe Water joins left.

6.5   Creamery on left bank. Road bridge (A709). Lochmaben 2km right, Lockerbie 3km left.
      After the bridge, river winds, and has marshy banks for next 7km.
      Hightae, then Smallholm hamlets on right bank.
      Scenery changes to wooded.

15.5 Island, and Linn Mill left. Remains of old broken weir in low water.

16   Road bridge.

17   St. Mungo's Church (historic) on left bank.

18   Mills on both banks.

19   Weir.

20.5 Water of Milk joins on left.

22.5 Hoddom bridge. Local paddlers tend to paddle from here to Annan.

24.5 Mein Water joins left.

26   Brydekirk bridge, village right. Weir just below bridge.

27   Large island.

28   Weir.

28.5 Annan by-pass bridge (A75).

29.5 Road bridge, on west side of the town of Annan. Egress. River becomes tidal here.

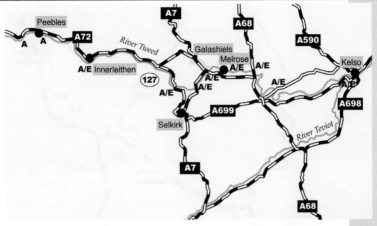

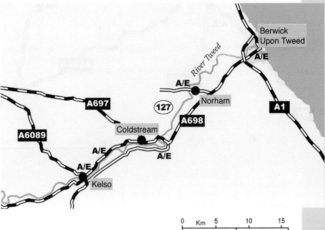

N

The Borders

127 River Tweed 225

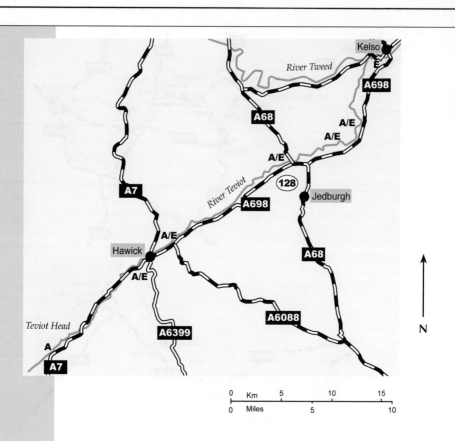

N

The Borders - continued

128   River Teviot. 229

The Borders

River Tweed 127

Grades Grade 1 and 2. Makerstoun lower rapid (-3).

Portages Some weirs might be portaged. They are mentioned in the text.

LENGTH **110km**
OS   **72-75**
GRADE **1/2(3-)**

Introduction The Tweed is the third of the original great Scottish rivers that were seen years ago as 'the Scottish trip', or the fourth if the Dee is counted as well. There has been a feeling over the last couple of decades that the Tweed carries nothing like the water it used to, and due to the nature of the Borders, this could well be due to greater agricultural abstraction. In low water, the river is a scrape down as far as Coldstream.

The Tweed valley has many historic associations, with castles and great houses. The upper valley is beautiful and wooded, the lower after Kelso more flat and agricultural.

The river is 110km from Peebles to Berwick, offering a trip of three or four days. The 'caulds' are basically gently-sloping weirs, many now broken down somewhat.

A trip could be split thus:

Peebles to Galashiels	32km
Galashiels to Kelso	30km
Kelso to Berwick	40km

Or:

From above Peebles to Innerleithen (riverside campsite)	16km
Innerleithen to Melrose	28km
Melrose to Kelso	27km
Kelso to Berwick	40km

Water Level Look over bridges. Driving up the valley will soon tell paddlers if the river is possible without a scrape.

The tributaries of the Tweed also suffer from a lack of water for most parts of the year, and are therefore mentioned in passing. They tend to be flat and stony, and 'flashy' in nature, coming up and going down very fast. None provide any great paddling

distance. The Teviot is in a different section because it does offer a
couple of days' paddling.

Access Bridge over Manor Water (231393), Peebles bridge
(250403), Innerleithen campsite (340366), Walkerburn bridge
(361369), Ashiesteel bridge (438351), Fairnilee bridge (459325), old
bridge off A7, with steps down (488323), Melrose ford (544345),
Leaderfoot (575346), Mertoun bridge (610320), Kelso riverside,
above weir (723343), A698 alongside river (8039), Coldstream
caravan site (845396), Norham bridge (891473) and Berwick riverside, below old bridge (997527).

Campsites & accommodation Peebles (not on the river), Innerleithen, Galashiels (4km away, up the Gala Water, a good centre
for touring the Borders), Melrose (off river), and Coldstream.
Rough camping is not available, or allowed down much of the
valley. Avoid agricultural land, and look for riverside woodland
or islands.

Description
The Tweed rises in the extreme south-west corner of the Borders,
just over the hill from Moffat, at Tweed's Well, a very obvious
spring near to the A701, Moffat to Edinburgh road. It can be
canoed or kayaked in high water from only a few kilometres
down the road, as the valley bottom is quite flat. At Tweedsmuir
road bridge is a considerable fall. A traditional place for starting trips was Stobo, about 25km downstream. However, in most
summers there is no chance of paddling loaded open canoes from
here, so distances are given from Peebles, where the river has
been joined by three small tributaries.

Km

0   Peebles bridge. Access downstream of bridge on south bank.
       Parking. The A72 road follows the river down the valley.

6   Cardrona, the 'new village'. New road bridge over.

12   Innerleithen bridge. Rapid. Traquair House to right. Village left.

13   Old railway bridge, and campsite left.

14   Walkerburn Cauld – can be lined down or portaged left.

15   Walkerburn bridge. Old woollen mill village left. Landing
       right below bridge.

23.5   Ashiesteel rapid, take right. Old slalom course. Footbridge.

27   Yair Cauld, usually shootable. Inspect next kilometre, as Fairnilee rapid comes after road bridge.

27.5   Fairnilee. Well-known slalom course. A nice rapid starting with a drop, main stream down left side. 200m of fast water. Lane and some parking,on left bank. Portage on left bank if desired.

30.5   Ettrick Water joins on right. River increases in size, two bridges, then faster water, with old concrete blocks in river. The Ettrick is a grade 2 paddle for 10km from the bridge below Ettrickbridge (Colin's bridge, 5km above Selkirk), down through Selkirk to join the Tweed. It is a grade 3 above this. There are some rocky rapids, a cauld at the junction of the Yarrow and a broken weir below Selkirk bridge. The Yarrow has a grade 3 gorge not far up from the confluence.

33   Abbotsford House (Sir Walter Scott's) to right. Landing and picnic place on left. Abbotsford bridge (main A6091 road). Borders General Hospital 3km right.
Gala Water joins left. Galashiels Town 2km left.

35.5   Road bridge.

37   Melrose Cauld. Steep and rocky, can be shot left when enough water. Portage left. Footbridge below, access/egress to Melrose right, Gattonside to left.

40.5   A68 road bridge. Old railway viaduct just before. Egress on right just above bridge, on to minor road. River Leader joins left. (The Leader gives a fast run of some 9km from the A68 bridge between Lauder and Earlston down a pleasant valley, near to the main road all the way).
Rapid just below confluence.
Scott's View, and Monument, very visible on hill on left bank for some distance.

45.5   Dryburgh footbridge. Dryburgh Abbey left.

46   Island, rock ledges and shallows below. Old campsite to left.

49   Merton Cauld. Shoot centre, or portage right. Bridge, B6404. Parking east side.
River broadens out, islands.

55.5   Rutherford Cauld. Left side to shoot, considerable waves, right at island below.

58   Makerstoun House on left bank signals approach to Mak-
      erstoun rapids, most difficult on Tweed. If water is low, this
      stretch will take some time. Upper and Middle Makerstoun
      rapids have a route through on the right sides, quite difficult
      to see at times, easier in high water. Lower Makerstoun
      rapid is appearing when the drop appears substantial ahead,
      and a row of cottages can be seen on right bank (no vehicle
      access down from these cottages!)

60   Lower Makerstoun rapid presents little problem for kayaks,
      but is tricky for open canoes… inspect. The usual route
      in medium water is down the extreme right side, down 4
      drops, with the last very narrow, requiring some skill. In
      high to very high water, there is a route down the left side of
      the river. River now quietens down considerably.

63   Floors Castle to left.

64   Kelso Cauld can be difficult, shoot on right in high water.
      Inspect.

      River Teviot joins right (See Route 128).

65   Road bridge. Most of town to left. Usual services. Cauld just
      after.

70.5 Banff Mill weirs. Four drops, all with fish shoots, water
      heavy if river is high.

75.5 Carham Cauld, usually a route to shoot.

77   Island, take right channel.

79.5 Cauld – shoot centre.

82   Approaching Coldstream. Caravan site to left.

82.5 Coldstream bridge. Town to left.

83.5 Cauld, route on right. River is now slow and deep, islands.

93   Road bridge, B6470, Norham village to right.

100.5 Union road bridge. River becomes tidal.

106.5 Berwick, road and rail bridges, town to left.

River Teviot 128

Introduction The Teviot is included as, alone amongst the Borders rivers, it offers a fair distance of good paddling (2 days), and is the most major of the Tweed tributaries. A trip down Teviot and Tweed would give 4 days of paddling, a lovely trip. It also almost follows main roads for much of the way.

The river rises in forest to the south-west of Hawick, and has been paddled from the aptly-named village of Teviothead. The river here is small, but possible in an open canoe in high water. The stretch of 4-5km through Hawick itself is the most tricky, but the rest is a grade 1/2, with pleasant and frequent rapids, (below Hawick section of maybe grade 3). The countryside is pretty all the way.

LENGTH **50km**
OS **74/79/80**
GRADE **1/2(3-)**

Water Level Judge from the level through Hawick. If enough water here, rest of river will be fine, but the higher reaches could still be shallow. They will need inspection.

Access Teviothead (408058), Martinshouse bridge, above Hawick (482134), campsite off A698 (534169), Ancrum bridge (639237), Kalemouth bridge (708274) and Kelso bridge (727336).

Campsites & accommodation Camping can be had just below Hawick, near Jedburgh on the River Jed, or as for River Tweed.

Description

Km

0   Teviothead. Small car park about 1km downstream of village, on left side alongside river. The A7 is a very busy road, take care. Overhanging trees down to Hawick.

4   River passes under the A7 to the south side.

7.5   Newmill. Minor road bridge. Pub and telephone to left.

11   Branxholm Bridgend - river passes under road to north side. Joined by Borthwick Water from left - flow increases.

12   Martin's bridge. Start of faster and shallower section.

13   Rugby pitches on left - keep right of island, many bushes and obstructions, especially supermarket trolleys. River becomes quite urban.

14   Hawick Cauld. Weir is safe to shoot, but avoid the salmon steps in the middle.

14.5   First road bridge.

15   Main Hawick road bridge, centre of town.
       River fast and straight, old woollen mills on banks.

17.5   Small weir, bend, bushes in river, (keep right), sharp bend, then 60m of rocky water with waves, small fall, stone bridge, and egress at campsite on right bank.

21   Road comes alongside river on left bank – egress, and some parking.

23   Road bridge, Denholm village on right bank.

26   Rule Water joins right. Long, slow and winding stretch now to A68 road.

31.5   Ale Water joins left.

32.5   A68 road bridge. Access upstream under old bridge. Jedburgh is 5km to right.
       Harestanes Estate both banks.

33.5   Easy sloping weir.

34.5   Footbridge, followed by broken-down cauld.

35   River Jed joins right. The Jed is a kayaking river in high water, with two high weirs in Jedburgh.

37   Nisbet road bridge, village left.

42   Kalemouth bridge, Kale Water joins right.
       Bend to left, then a broken weir, followed by trees.

43   Island.

44   Weir, small drop, easy to shoot.

45   Old railway bridge, now a footpath.

45.5   Weir.

46   Weir.

48.5   Long, straight stretch, followed by broken cauld. Castle on high left bank, with River Tweed on the other side.
       Sharp bend to right heralds islands, rocky water, road bridge, a weir, and the last stretch down to the Tweed. This bit of river used in the past as a slalom site.

50   Junction with River Tweed.

Cross-Scotland Routes

Cross-Scotland Routes

A   Laxford Bridge to Bonar Bridge . . 234
B   Inverkirkaig to Bonar Bridge. . . 235
C   Loch Maree to Conon Bridge   . 236
D   Great Glen (Caledonian Canal) . 236
E   Loch Nevis to Great Glen 239
F   Loch Morar to Great Glen 240
G   Kinlochleven to Perth 240
H   Loch Long to Stirling 242
I   Loch Long to River Forth and
     Stirling 243
J   Glasgow to Edinburgh 243
K   Solway Firth to Berwick. 244

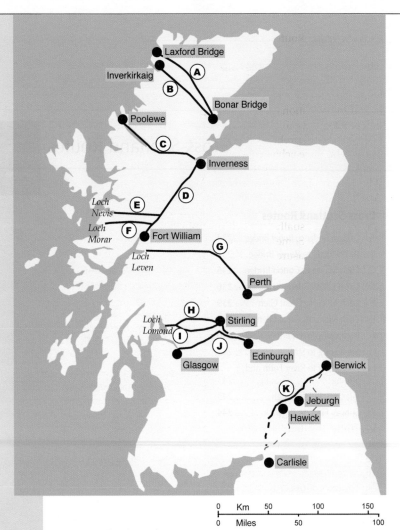

Cross-Scotland Routes

A   Laxford Bridge to Bonar Bridge 234
B   Inverkirkaig to Bonar Bridge . 235
C   Loch Maree to Conon Bridge 236
D   Great Glen (Caledonian Canal) 236
E   Loch Nevis to Great Glen . . 239
F   Loch Morar to Great Glen. . . 240

G   Kinlochleven to Perth 240
H   Loch Long to Stirling. 242
I   Loch Long to River Forth
     and Stirling. 243
J   Glasgow to Edinburgh 243
K   Solway Firth to Berwick 244

Cross-Scotland Routes

All of the routes in this section are quite long and serious expeditions, although the two 'low level' routes have the advantage of being both sheltered from the worst of the weather, and being nearer to habitation and help. The canal route across the Central Belt of Scotland can also be quite urban in places, and the Great Glen passage is probably the most-paddled holiday in Scotland. Those who have achieved it will also have a quiet smile when remembering heavy weather on Loch Ness, when this guide says it has 'shelter from bad weather'!

Apart from those two, the other routes across Scotland can be quite a challenge, with boggy portages, heat and midges in high summer, and usually a stiff climb up from the west coast to the watershed. Some are indeed quite mad, and are not recommended for pleasure!

Paddlers are warned that in most places, the terrain means that canoe trolleys can't be used for portaging, and that it can be treacherous underfoot. Lining up or down watercourses can also be well-nigh impossible. A best plan would be for paddlers to carry all their gear in rucksacks, and therefore be free to carry canoes or kayaks. If not, an expedition might be forced into several journeys over the most problematic stretches.

Whilst the carrying of mobile phones can be a safety measure, as can be back-up crews, please remember that mobile phone masts are not erected in the mountains on the watershed, where help might be most needed. Signal strength is not assured. Finally and cheerfully, Scotland is famous for very changeable weather, which can quite well mean snow showers on midsummer day. All in all, the lesson is that expedition groups must be self-sufficient, carrying all necessary food, water and clothing.

The routes are described from the north of Scotland to the south, and only bare details are given. Proper planning with maps must allow for distances, features and obstacles. Routes through peat bogs, and river features such as weirs and walkways etc. do change over time. Follow the Scottish Access Code with regard to rough camping, take only photos and leave only footprints.

A Laxford Bridge to Bonar Bridge

LEN. **72.5**km

OS **9/15/16**

GRADE   **2**

Introduction A route commencing in one of the most spectacular parts of the north, with views of the quartzite Arkle and Foinaven to the east. Loch Laxford is a nice place to start; the height of this route is not a problem, a main road following all of the way, but the long easterly drag down Loch Shin to the east is not one of Scotland's finest bits of scenery.

Description Laxford Bridge – portage east up A838 4.5km to Laxford Lodge (the River Laxford is a nice grade 3/4 river); Loch Stack is a lovely 3.5km to the end, with Ben Stack a beautiful conical mountain to the south; 1km up the road to Loch nan Ealachan, under bridge to Loch More, which is 1km long.

3.5km up the road to Loch Merkland, (you cross the watershed at 144m); Loch Merkland is 4.5km, and now you may be able to paddle downhill on the Merkland River (some rapids), 2km. Loch a Ghriama (2.5km) follows, an offshoot of Loch Shin, then this main and very long loch of 27km. Loch Shin does feel like it's never going to end, and it has relatively few features. Very much a fishing loch, you will meet many small boats.

Lairg is a welcome break, the only town on this route, and then a choice – a long road portage, or the River Shin – 12km by road to Invershin Station, on the Kyle of Sutherland, or an attempt at parts of the river, with often no water, including the Falls of Shin. Getting in and out of the river gorge is not easy.

Then follows 5km of tidal water to Bonar Bridge.

Other important points

Total distance: 72.5km.

Time required: Probably 4 days.

Inverkirkaig to Bonar Bridge B

Introduction This is a difficult, and not to be recommended route. It was paddled to join up two quite reasonable canoeing areas, the Inverpolly Nature Reserve area in the west, north of Ullapool, and the River Oykel/Kyle of Sutherland route in the east.

LEN. **67.5**km
OS **15/16/21**
GRADE **1/2/3**

Description From Inverkirkaig, a few miles south of Lochinver, the route goes up the River Kirkaig (see Scottish White Water) valley. The valley is beautiful, but the portage is fairly tough, some 3km to the Falls, and a further 1km to the Fionn Loch, up an often wet, muddy, and stony track.

Then follows a lovely 11km through Fionn Loch, the connecting short river, and Loch Veyatie to the waterfall at the top. 3km round to the Ledmore River which is flat, and can usually be paddled upstream 4.5km to Loch Borralan. The idea of the route then ends up with a problem, as the burn coming down is impossible to line. It is a portage of 4.5km to the Allt Eileag (now in Scottish WW, grade 3), over the watershed, access to the Oykel. When I did this, we had no idea of the steepness of the river and ended up in a difficult and hard portage (mostly) 1.5km from the road down to the Oykel. The other alternative is a portage of 12km to Lubcroy. The river has a slow 8km down to Lubcroy – rapids from grade 1 to grade 3, fast if one has nerves in high water, otherwise some portages and wading.

Lubcroy to a point by the river, alongside a Highland Council Roads depot, 2km. A portage along the road for 1km to Oykel Bridge and hotel avoids a white water stretch including the Falls of Oykel.

The paddler will be pleased to know that from here, it is all straightforward to the sea at Bonar Bridge (tidal before this point), 28km. (See Route 026).

Other important points
Total distance: 67.5km.
Time required: Probably 4 days at least.

C Loch Maree to Conon Bridge

LEN. **85.5km**
OS **20/25/26**

GRADE   **1-2**

Outline Loch Maree, River Bran and River Conon to Conon Bridge.

Introduction This is a reported route, second-hand from writing on a bothy wall, with only initials, not a full name. As the start and finish have been done many times, there is no reason to suspect it.

Description See Route 022, for Loch Maree. The loch is portaged alongside the River Ewe, up from Poolewe, for 1km, then Loch Maree is 21km long. A portage of 3km up to Kinlochewe is followed by a further portage of 8km over the watershed to Loch a Chroisg.
See Route 029 for the rest of the route down the lochs to the River Bran and on to the River Conon.

Other important points
Total distance: 85.5km.
Time required: Probably 5 days, so as not to hurry Loch Maree, to account for the long central portage, and for the lower portages.

D Great Glen (Caledonian Canal)

LENGTH **92km**
OS **26/34/41**

GRADE   -

Introduction This is deservedly a very popular route across Scotland, but it is still quite possible to paddle for three or four days and not see another canoe outside of the midsummer holiday period. It is a voyage at nearly sea level, with great scenery all the way, and the safety of a canal with traffic and a main road. It is still possible, however, to find both places for stops on the way where there is peace and quiet and rough camping spots. The latter are, however, becoming less easy to find.
British Waterways control the canal, and a very good website has many practical details about the canal (www.scottishcanals.com).

Description The route is 96.6km long (60 miles), of which 35.4km (22miles) is man-made. The Caledonian Canal is one of the great waterways of the world, sharing characteristics with both the Gota Canal in Sweden and the Rideau Canal in Canada, both of which it is twinned with.

Designed by Thomas Telford, the canal was built between 1803 and 1822. It has four aqueducts over burns, (one being the canoe-able though small Loy), 29 locks, and 10 bridges.

A 'normal' time for a passage by canoe is three days, which can obviously be extended with sightseeing. Large boats using the locks are told it will take them a minimum of 14 hours over two days. The locks only work during a normal working day, 8.00 until 6.00pm in summer, and are worked by BW staff. Plan to portage around the locks, some of which are long flights, although you might just be able to attach yourself to a friendly motor cruiser.

The route is described from south to north, as this is the usual way of the prevailing wind, but it can change! The lochs all can build up large waves in high wind, so be prepared to either stop, or to paddle close to one of the banks.

There are various formal campsites along the glen, some on the water, and some places are mentioned as having rough camping possibilities.

Km

0   Fort William/Corpach.
      The Neptune's Staircase series of locks stretch for 2.5km.

12.5 Gairloch swing bridge. Entrance to Loch Lochy. River Lochy leaves on right, 250m, and then the River Arkaig enters on left after 3.5km.
      Loch Lochy is 15km long.

27.5 The loch narrows, yacht moorings on right, then on left.

28   Laggan locks. Small village and B&Bs to right.

30.5 Laggan swing bridge. Entrance to Loch Oich.
      Loch Oich is wooded and extremely pretty, 6km long.
      Great Glen Water Park on right, accommodation and camping.

34   On left side, Invergarry Castle, Glengarry Hotel, and then the mouth of River Garry. Just after this on left, possibilities for camping in marshy woodland.
      This loch has buoyage for larger boats as it is relatively shallow and narrow.

36.5 End of loch, Bridge of Oich, road swing-bridge. River Oich leaves left over weir.

37.5 Collochy Lock.

40.5   Kytra Lock.

44   Fort Augustus locks. Plan to have a break here, as the carry down these locks will leave you exhausted. Often a busy place, where the world stops to watch people in boats hitting each other and the lock walls. Town with shops and cafes etc. Exit to Loch Ness, a wondrous sight, as it stretches to the horizon, all 36km of it!

51   Rubha Ban campsite on left bank.

52   Invermoriston to left.

60   Foyers village to right.

64   Inverfarigaig to right.

69   Urquhart Castle on left bank, followed by Urquhart Bay on left. Camping possibilities here, much wooded and marshy ground.
On right side of loch, many picnic sites.

75.5   Camp and caravan site on right bank.

78   Tore Point, loch narrows.

80.5   Lochend village on left side.
Loch Ness becomes the narrower Loch Dochfour.

82.5   River Ness leaves right.

83.5   Dochgarroch village left. Campsite.

89.5   Canal leaves river – two campsites.

91   Muirtown Locks.

92   Canal leaves Muirtown Basin into the sea.

Loch Nevis to Great Glen E

Outline Loch Nevis, River Carnoch, Loch Quoich and River Garry to Great Glen.

LEN.   **131**km
OS **33/34/26**
GRADE   **1-2**

Introduction This is again a reported route, a variation of the Great Glen, using the Garry system from the west coast, but with a very tough carry over the western watershed.

Description The route commences from the head of Loch Nevis, with a paddle in from either Mallaig, or along Loch Morar (see Routes 043 and 044). The route is from the north-east exit from the loch at Camusory, up the River Carnach. The river might be paddled or lined for a distance up, but after 2km or so the gradient steepens. It is 7km up to a small loch, the 1km Lochan nam Breac, then a final 1.5km rocky dribble to Loch Quoich, over 200m climb vertically.
The lochs of Glens Quoich and Garry then follow (see Route 049), for 36km to the River Garry, to be portaged, 5km, as far as Loch Oich.
The Great Glen - Route D above is then followed to Inverness (58km).

Other important points
Total distance: 129km (Loch Morar route).
                     131km (Loch Nevis route from Mallaig).

Time required: This must take at least 6 days, and could take considerably more. The terrain for the main portage is very hard, and this route is one of the longest across Scotland.

F Loch Morar to Great Glen

LEN. **128**km
OS **33/40/41**
GDE. **2+(4+)**

Outline Loch Morar, Glen Pean, Loch Arkaig to Loch Lochy and Great Glen.

Introduction This is again a variation of the route above, with the ascent made from the head of Loch Morar, instead of Nevis.

Description The approach is as Route 044, and then Glen Pean is taken almost due east from the south-east end of the loch. The unnamed glen has a 2.5km climb up to the bealach, to a height of 120m, and is noteworthy for the giant rock, 'Noah's Ark', which guards the entry to Glen Pean. The burn down here is small for 4.5km, passing through a large lochan on the way down. It is then joined by numerous tiny water courses near a bothy and a ruin, and becomes a larger river that may be paddled. It is a further 5.5km to Loch Arkaig.
Loch Arkaig (Route 051) is 19km long, and the 2km River Arkaig (one portage, grade 4+), leads down to Loch Lochy in the Great Glen. From this point to Inverness is 76km.

Other important points
Total distance: 128km.
Time required: As for the route just above, although there is a longer distance of easier terrain, probably 5-6 days.

G Kinlochleven to Perth

LEN. **128**km
OS **41-43/53**
GDE. **2/3(4)**

Outline Kinlochleven to Perth via Blackwater Reservoir, Rannoch Moor, Gaur, Rannoch, Tummel and Tay.

Introduction This is a very hard, though rewarding cross-country route, at 325m height, the highest route of this group. It also has some of the toughest portages.

Description The trip starts at Kinlochleven at the head of Loch Leven (Route 056), off Loch Linnhe. There is immediately a horrific climb, from sea level up to the Blackwater Reservoir, the highest the expedition will go, in just 6.5km. The one saving grace of this path, starting as a forest track, is that it becomes a concrete cover over the outflow from the dam after 2.5km, and the canoe trolley will hum along over this. (This fact was kept secret by several writers of the route in the past). This climb will take half a day, and the dam provides a greatly scenic campsite, surrounded by mountains, so using a first afternoon or evening for this part is maybe a good plan, as recovery time will be needed.

The Blackwater Reservoir is 12.5km long, and the height often means that a sail across here is quite likely in the prevailing westerlies.

The problems really start at the eastern end. It is only about 6.5km as the crow flies east, then south to Rannoch Station, but the route-finding and terrain can make grown men weep! The river is shallow, rock-strewn and winding, and so any lining-up can be forgotten. The only answer is to carry the canoe or kayak over uneven ground, trying to remember where one is going. After a time, the railway line comes invitingly near to the north, but beware – it is first of all illegal to walk on the line, and secondly, you might know the times of the passenger trains but you won't know when freight trains are coming! There are also snow tunnels here – bad to meet a train in.

Once reaching Rannoch Station, you are on the way downhill, with the hotel and café beckoning.

The next obstacle is that, after paddling on to Dubh Lochan and Loch Laidon, 1km, and finding the river exit, the Garbh Ghaoir - 3km, can be a mite difficult. Immediately, two grade 2/3 rapids follow, the second under the railway bridge, and then an appreciable drop as a good grade 3 takes you 800m down to Loch Eigheach. At least you get 2km of flat paddling, then over the dam (either side) down on to the road to Loch Rannoch. The River Gaur poses a problem. It has some easy water, but one grade 4 rapid, seen after 2km down the road, and also at least two places of rocky grade 3. The only real solution is to walk – a portage of 4km to Bridge of Gaur. At this bridge, access can be had onto the end of the river just before it joins Loch Rannoch.

The rest of the route is covered in Routes 083, 084 and 092.

Other important points

The distances are:

Kinlochleven to Rannoch Station – 26km.
Rannoch Station to Pitlochry – 57.5km.
Pitlochry to Perth – 54.5km.
Total distance: 138km.
Time required: Could be done by the very fit in 3 days (the Tay is very fast), but a more sensible target is 4-5 days.

H Loch Long to Stirling

LENGTH **63km**
OS   **56/57**
GDE. **1/2(3-)**

Outline Lochs Long, Lomond, Arklet, Katrine, and Venachar to Stirling.

Introduction This is a lovely route, but at the time of writing 'illegal' because boating is not allowed on Loch Katrine, being Glasgow's water supply. This is due to change in 2006, maybe, with the completion of a new treatment works nearer Glasgow. However, the route has been completed, and was probably first done in the 1950s. Possibly the sight of the tourist steamer on the loch proved too much of a temptation. The middle sections of small river and loch can also be very dry.

Description Loch Long and Loch Lomond are covered in Routes 071 and 072. After 8km from Arrochar, over the portage and up Loch Lomond to Inversnaid, it is a portage of 2km to Loch Arklet, and this loch is 4km long. The road over to Loch Katrine is 1.5km down to Stronachlachar pier. Loch Katrine is 9km down to its end at the road in Achray Water, though the dam at the south-west corner is likely to be dry, and is also heavily wooded. The loch has some lovely campsites on the wooded banks.
The portage along the road to Loch Achray is only 1.5km, and Loch Achray is 2km long. From here the route is Route 108 down to Stirling. Once on the River Teith progress is a lot faster.

Other important points
Total distance: 63km.
Time required: 3 days (probably including an overnight from Inversnaid to Loch Achray).

Loch Long to River Forth and Stirling

Outline Lochs Long, Lomond, Arklet, Chon, and Ard to River Forth and Stirling.

LENGTH **82**km
OS **56/57**
GRADE **1**

Introduction This is a variation of Route H above and has also the current bar to paddling the Lochs Arklet and Chon. The other disadvantage is the tedious River Forth, but the route does cross Scotland!

Description Loch Long and Loch Lomond, Routes 071 and 072. As above, 16km to the eastern end of Loch Arklet. Then the route turns south, portage of 4km to Loch Chon, and the loch provides 3.5km of paddling through a small river to Loch Dhu. Off on to the road again for 2.5km down to Loch Ard. These two sections of road need care in the summer as they are very busy (perhaps best to do the portages in an evening). Loch Ard, however, is a delight. Enjoy it because then the River Forth commences, pleasant to Aberfoyle. For River Forth, see Route 109.

Other important points
Total distance: 82km.

Time required: 3 days (more if you take your time on the Forth).

Glasgow to Edinburgh

Outline Glasgow to Edinburgh, via the Forth and Clyde Canal, and Union Canal.

LEN.   **103**km
OS **64/65/66**
GRADE   -

Description These two canals are described in Routes 112 and 113. Planning would have to include an overnight stop, either as described for rough camping or by leaving the canal, or even by staying somewhere comfortable, possibly near Falkirk if going west to east.

Other important points
Total distance: 103km.
Time required: 2 days minimum.

K Solway Firth to Berwick

LEN. **103**km
OS **Text**
GDE. **1/2(3-)**

Outline Solway Firth via Teviot and Tweed to Berwick.

OS Sheets 85,79,80,74 and 75.

Introduction   This is the craziest route by far, and came out of a bet the author had… it happened years ago just after a couple of open canoe luminaries had circumnavigated Wales (work that out!).

Description I had the idea of paddling and sailing around the south of Scotland. From Edinburgh to Glasgow was easy enough, but the border presented a new problem. So, one day I and a companion set out, luckily with a support crew. We sailed up the 24km of the Solway from Southerness, west of Dumfries on a high flood tide (this was the best bit), and managed to paddle up the Border Esk as far as Longtown (8km from the river mouth). Trying to paddle/line up/drag the canoe further up proved rather difficult, and so after another 7km left the river below Canonbie.
We then gave in with exhaustion, and portaged the canoes (by car) the 33km up to Teviothead, but then did make the whole journey down the Teviot and Tweed.
For the Teviot and Tweed, see Routes 127 and 128.

Other important points
Total distance: 140km.
Time required: Endless, but at least 5 days.

Index

A

Achray, Loch. 189
Add, River 97
Affric, Loch. 54
Alsh, Loch 62
Annan, River 221
Arkaig, Loch. 81
Ard, Loch 191
Auchencairn Bay 219
Avich, Loch 93
Avon, River. 195
Awe, Loch 92
Ayr, River 201

B

Bà, Loch. 86
Balquhidder to Loch Lubnaig 187
Balvaig. 187
Beauly, River 50
Beinn a Mheadhoin, Loch 54
Brighouse Bay 212
Broom, Little Loch 39
Bute, Isle of and Nearby Lochs 103

C

Caledonian Canal. 236
Carron, Loch 61
Clyde, Firth of. 111
Clyde, Upper 206
Clyde, Lower 207
Conon, River and Upper Lochs 49
Cononish 148
Craignish, Loch 96
Creran, Loch. 87
Crinan Canal 97
Crinan, Loch 97
Crowlin Islands. 61

D

Daimh, Loch 145
Dean Water 171
Dee, River 132, 217
Deveron, River 128
Devon, River 193
Dionard, River 24
Dochart 148
Don, River 130
Doon, Loch 203
Dornoch Firth. 45
Duich, Loch 62
Duich, Loch to Loch Hourn 63
Durness, Kyle of 23

E

Earn, River 161
Eden, River. 176
Eilt, Loch 73
Endrick Water. 112
Eriboll, Loch 23
Ericht, Loch 123
Ericht, Lower 161
Etive, Loch 90
Ewe, Loch. 40

F

Forth and Clyde Canal 197
Forth, River. 191
Fillan 148
Findhorn, Lower 122
Findhorn, Upper. 120
Fionn Loch. 37
Fleet, Loch 46
Fyne, Loch 102

G

Gairloch, Loch 41
Gare Loch 104
Garry, Loch 80
Garry, Upper River 80
Gatehouse of Fleet 212
Glasgow to Edinburgh 243
Glass, River 50
Goil, Loch 104
Great Glen (Caledonian Canal). . . . 236
Gruinard Bay 39

H

Handa Island 26
Holy Loch 104
Hourn, Loch 64

I

Inchard, Loch 25
Inverkirkaig to Bonar Bridge 235
Inverpolly Lochs, The 31
Isla, Lower River. 158
Isla, Upper River 156

J K

Ken, Loch 217
Ken, River. 217
Kinlochleven to Perth 240
Kirkcudbright Bay. 212
Kishorn, Loch 61
Kylesku Area. 29

L

Laggan, Loch 83
Laidon, Loch 86
Laxford Bridge to Bonar Bridge. . . . 234
Laxford, Loch 25
Leven, Loch 85, 181
Leven, River 111, 181
Linnhe, Loch 85
Lochinver. 30
Lochy, Loch 81
Lochy, River 82
Lomond, Loch 109, 111
Long, Loch 62, 104, 111
Long, Loch to R. Forth and Stirling . 243
Long, Loch to Stirling 242
Luce Bay 211
Lubnaig, Loch 187
Lunan Water. 172
Lyon, Loch 146
Lyon, Lower River. 147
Lyon, Upper River. 146

M

Maree, Loch .40
Maree, Loch to Conon Bridge 236
Melfort, Loch and Nearby Islands. 94
Moidart, Loch 73, 74
Monar, Loch 52
Monar, Loch - West to the Sea 53
Morar, Loch to Great Glen 240
Morar, Loch 66, 67
Moriston, River. 55
Mullardoch, Loch. 54

N

Nairn, River 119
Naver, Loch 21
Naver, River 21
Ness, Loch 56
Ness, River. 56
Nevis, Loch to Great Glen 239
Nevis, Loch 66, 67
Nith Estuary 220
Nith, Lower 220
North Esk, Lower 166

O

Oich, Loch 81
Orchardton Bay 219
Orchy, Lower 91
Oykel, Lower River 45

P Q R

Polly, River. 37
Quoich, Loch 80
Rannoch, Loch 139
Rannoch Moor. 86
Rannoch Station 86
Rough Firth. 219

S

Shee Water, Upper 160
Shiel, Loch 68, 73
Shiel, River. 73
Shin, Loch 44
Sionascaig, Loch 32
Solway Firth to Berwick. 244
South Esk, Lower 169
South Esk, Upper 168
Spean, Loch 83
Spey, River 123
Stoer 30
Stirling 243
Summer Isles, The 38
Sunart, Loch 75
Sutherland, Kyle of 45
Sween, Loch 98

T

Tarbert, West Loch 99
Tay, Firth of 155
Tay, Loch 150
Tay, River 151
Tayvallich and Loch Sween. 98
Teith, River 189
Teviot, River 229
Thurso, Lower. 20
Thurso, Middle. 20
Thurso, Upper 19
Tongue, Kyle of. 22
Torridon, Loch 42
Treig, Loch 84
Tummel, Loch 140
Tummel, Lower River 140
Tweed, River. 225

U V W X Y Z

Union Canal. 196
Venachar, Loch. 189
Veyatie, Loch 37
West Loch Tarbert. 99
Whithorn, Isle of and Garlieston 211